Stephen Reel has done a masterful job of "focusing" in on what is really important in life – Jesus Christ. As I read *Clear Focus,* I was both convicted and challenged in my everyday walk with the Lord. Stephen leads the reader to desire to know Christ deeper and out of that desire to love and serve others as Christ did while here on earth. He accomplishes this by skillfully telling accounts in Scripture in a way that makes the Bible come alive and the reader thinking he is actually there taking part in the work of Christ. I know that he wrote this book primarily for Christian school educators, but I believe this is a must-read for every single Christian.

Dr. Glen Schultz
Author of *Kingdom Education*

Dr. Stephen Reel takes us back to the essential focus we need in Christian school ministry by helping us to refocus on "who" so that the tyranny of "what" does not rob us of the joy of ministry. This book is full of practical application and the Word of God permeates every topic. This is a must-read for anyone ministering in Christian schooling.

Dr. Daniel Egeler
President of the Association of Christian Schools International (ACSI)

Stephen Reel uses Biblical teaching and his personal experiences as a Christian school educator to renew our perspective on what really matters most in Christian education—a clear focus on Jesus and those He calls us to serve.

Dr. Bill Jones
President of Columbia International University

*Clear Focus* is the call to regenerate the thinking of Christian school teachers and leaders around the world. It is the best book written for the Christian school movement in the last 25 years!

Dr. Janet Lowrie Nason
Advisor to CEO of IPEKA Christian Schools

Dr. Stephen Reel inspires us to see ministry through the eyes of Jesus. In a world full of important distractions, the whats of life, Stephen encourages Christians to fix our gaze on life's Who and whos. Through powerful Scriptural insights and his own life stories, Stephen calls us to intentional and relational living, connecting daily to our Lord and His people. I am among the many whos refocused by the reading of this essential work.

Dr. Todd Marrah
Headmaster of Tree of Life Christian School

# CLEAR FOCUS

Rediscovering the Most Important Aspect
of Christian School Ministry

Stephen G. Reel, PhD

WESTBOW°
PRESS
A DIVISION OF THOMAS NELSON
& ZONDERVAN

WestBow Press books may be ordered through booksellers or by contacting:

WestBow Press
A Division of Thomas Nelson & Zondervan
1663 Liberty Drive
Bloomington, IN 47403
www.westbowpress.com
1 (866) 928-1240

ISBN: 978-1-4908-8318-2 (sc)
ISBN: 978-1-4908-8320-5 (hc)
ISBN: 978-1-4908-8319-9 (e)

Library of Congress Control Number: 2015908997

Print information available on the last page.

WestBow Press rev. date: 06/29/2015

*This book is dedicated to my best friend
and love of my life, Melanie.
Her clear focus on Jesus and on our family
is a constant inspiration to me.*

# CONTENTS

# ACKNOWLEDGEMENTS

When I conducted a search of the most commonly used words in *Clear Focus,* the number one result was Jesus! I rejoice in Christ alone *so that in everything he might have the supremacy* (Col. 1:18). It is with a grateful heart I acknowledge my Lord and Savior, Jesus Christ, without Whom I could never have clear focus.

I am also grateful for a lifetime of wonderful teachers and mentors who have instilled in me a love for learning. I will always remember my fifth grade teacher, Miss Ramsey, who told my class that one day she wanted to read the books that I would write. Her confidence in me often sustained me when I had doubts about writing a book. This is also a tangible reminder of the powerful result of a teacher's clear focus on her students.

I want to thank the members of the Southside Christian School Board of Directors for all of their support for this project. I am especially grateful for the gift of time they gave me to write. Special recognition goes to Dr. Jim and Becky Baucum for the use of their beautiful lake house, allowing me to truly have clear focus during the writing process.

I am especially indebted to the faculty/staff of Southside Christian School for their exceptional modeling of clear focus in their daily ministry to their students and families. They were my inspiration for this book. I am also appreciative of the faculty/staff of Ipeka Christian School in Jakarta, Indonesia, for granting me the privilege to share many of the concepts of *Clear Focus* in their professional development sessions. Their encouragement spurred me on to completion.

I am very thankful for the copy editing skill and assistance of Denise Loock with Lightning Editing Services. Thanks also to Jennifer Morris and the entire WestBow Press team for their wonderful support.

Finally, I want to express my sincere gratitude to my family and friends who have supported me throughout this journey. There is really no way to quantify how much their confidence, words of encouragement, and enthusiastic support has meant to me. I am standing upon their shoulders.

# INTRODUCTION

---

Who, what, when, where, why, and how? We ask these essential questions about almost everything, rattling them off in a single breath as if they have equal weight. I suggest we change our perspective. The primary question we should ask is "who?" The other questions are secondary. They should support the first question:

- What for who?
- When for who?
- Where for who?
- Why for who?
- How for who?

When we focus intently on *who,* we begin to escape the tyranny of *what,* which steals the joy from our lives and service. Jesus perfectly modeled this for us. Follow Him through any day of His ministry, and you will see His focus is always on a who. Ours should be too.

My sincere prayer for you as you read *Clear Focus* is that you will be able to rediscover this most important aspect of Christian school ministry.

**About the Cover:** Jesus said, "I tell you, open your eyes and look at the fields! They are ripe for harvest" (John 4:35). This stalk of wheat reminds us that every person God brings into our lives is worthy of our clear focus.

# CHAPTER 1

# Focus

*Let your eyes look directly forward, and*
*your gaze be straight before you.*
Proverbs 4:25 (ESV)

Focus.

If we are honest, the word *focus* seems intimidating and tiresome. It takes hard work and intentionality to focus on something. It does not help when we are constantly surrounded by sensory overload every waking minute of the day—a frenetic barrage of multiple images, sounds, words, and symbols, all vying for our attention—and that is just on our smart phones. This digital bombardment, combined with an assortment of other visual and auditory interruptions, is a constant competitor of any person we encounter. Thankfully, someone coined the word *multitasking* to help ease our guilt and justify the insanity of it all.

In the blur of this full-fledged assault on our minds, focus seems nearly impossible. Yet we recognize that excellence requires focus. We respect and appreciate the focus of people such as Bill Gates and Steve Jobs because their commitment to technology revolutionized the way we live our lives. Or how about the tremendous mental and physical focus of Olympic athletes? We admire the Swiss for their watches, each one fashioned with precision and integrity. One of my cousins is an accomplished architectural artist who is commissioned to draw, in intricate detail, famous buildings such as the Biltmore House. He often works on a single square inch of a drawing for weeks to ensure every line and shadow perfectly matches the original.[1] What focus!

We expect that kind of focus from those who serve us—from a cashier in a grocery store or a waiter at a restaurant. We grow impatient if our servers are multitasking while attending to our needs. Would any of us want to have an unfocused brain surgeon operating on our child? Of course not. We expect a laser-like focus on something that significant. But sadly, we often lack the discipline and practice necessary to achieve it ourselves.

In Christian school ministry, we have been given the privilege to serve as skilled artisans for our Lord, equipping our students—His masterpieces created in Christ Jesus—to do the good things He designed for them to do (Ephesians 2:10). So focus is not optional; it is required.

Give focus a try. Take a moment, close your eyes, and try to focus on something for a moment or two. Do not skip this important exercise. No peeking. And do not fall asleep while you do it.

Focus.

Back so soon? That was fast. So how many of us would be willing to admit that we could not remain focused on something for even one minute? Sad, huh? Why is it so difficult? We could blame all the distractions since there are certainly plenty of them. But I suggest that even in a sound-proof room without any electronic devices, noises, and images, without practice and serious mental concentration, we would not be much more effective at focusing on something—even with our eyes closed. We are prone to engage in mental gymnastics, so we often become as distracted with rabbit-trail thoughts with our eyes closed as we do when our eyes are open. If we are honest, much of our prayer life is like this. Ouch!

Try something different. Close your eyes and focus on a person whom you love for a moment or two. Again, do not skip this or you will miss the main point of the chapter.

That was easier, right? Maybe your mind, like mine, was flooded with joyful thoughts and memories of that person—how beautiful she looks when the sunlight catches her face at just the right angle with a little sweep of hair falling across her face, how those deep blue eyes sparkle, how she hums when she is happy as she prepares dinner for our family, how she looks at her children with such deep compassion when they are hurting, how the sound of her voice almost sings when she is proud of me, and how she sinks into my arms after a long day and sighs, "I need you." Ahhh.

Forgive me. I got lost when I focused on the love of my life, my bride of thirty years, Melanie. Perhaps you did that too as you thought about someone dear to you. And if we added a few visual or auditory cues, we could probably focus intently on that person for a longer period of time.

The key? We are focusing on a who.

That should not surprise us. Our Creator designed us that way. In fact, we were designed to focus on Him. God is the ultimate Who of our existence. Moses wrote, *If . . . you seek the LORD your God, you will find him if you seek him with all your heart and with all your soul* (Deut. 4:29). The psalmist asked, *Whom have I in heaven but you? And earth has nothing I desire besides you. My flesh and my heart may fail, but God is the strength of my heart and my portion forever* (Ps. 73:25-26). God is the object of our eternal focus. Isaiah wrote, *You will keep in perfect peace all who trust in you, all whose thoughts are fixed on you!* (Isa. 26:3 NLT). Another psalmist wrote, *I lift my eyes to you, O God, enthroned in heaven. We keep looking to the LORD our God for his mercy, just as servants keep their eyes on their master, as a slave girl watches her mistress for the slightest signal* (Ps. 123:1-2 NLT).

No wonder Scripture instructs us to fix our eyes on Jesus, *the author and finisher of our faith* (Heb. 12:2 NKJV). He is the *image of the invisible God* (Col. 1:15). And His light, shining in our heart, gives us *the light of the knowledge of God's glory displayed in the face of Christ* (2 Cor. 4:6).

The words of songwriter Helen H. Lemmel are fitting:

> Turn your eyes upon Jesus,
> Look full in His wonderful face,
> And the things of earth will grow strangely dim,
> In the light of His glory and grace.

The inspiration for these lyrics came from the writings of author and artist Lilias Trotter. Her love and calling for missionary service to the Muslims of Algeria caused her to lay down her love for art to more perfectly focus on Jesus. The following is an excerpt from her tract, *Which Passion Will Prevail?*

> Never has it been so easy to live in half a dozen harmless worlds at once—art, music, social science, games, motoring, the following of some profession, and so on. And between them we run the risk of drifting about, the good hiding the best. It is easy to find out whether our lives are focused, and if so, where the focus lies. Where do our thoughts settle when consciousness comes back in the morning? Where do they swing back when the pressure is off during the day? Dare to have it out with God, and ask Him to show you whether or not all is focused on Christ and His Glory. Turn your soul's vision to Jesus, and look and look at Him, and a strange dimness will come over all that is apart from Him.[2]

Once we understand the significance of focusing on the true Who of our existence, we can then begin to understand how to properly focus on other whos in our life. People matter to God, and because of this, they must matter to us. In effect, they deserve our focus because they have His focus. As we focus on the Lord, we will soon learn that the focus of His attention is on His precious creations, made in His image and likeness. We will be captivated by the fact that He loves each and every one of these replicas of Himself. Although they are marred and broken from the devastating effects of sin, He longs for them to be fully restored. He weeps over them with compassion. He desires for them to be back in close fellowship with the Trinity.

As we watch for the slightest signal from our Master, we will soon realize He wants to use us as His agents of mercy to others. Hebrews 7:25 states that Jesus is *able to save completely those who come to God through him, because he always lives to intercede for them.* Jesus longs to rescue, redeem, and restore those He loves. And He wants to use us in the process.

Let me illustrate. Think back to a time before you were a Christian. How did you come to know and understand the mercy of God? How did you realize that He wanted to rescue you from your sinful condition? Did you one day come to your senses and seek God through remorseful prayer and Bible reading? Maybe. But it is more likely that someone came to you with the message of God's love. God sent that person as an agent of mercy. That person was focused on a who—you. Consider Paul's description in Romans 10:

> *As Scripture says ... "Everyone who calls on the name of the Lord will be saved." How, then, can they call on the one they have not believed in? And how can they believe in the one of whom they have not heard? And how can they hear without someone preaching to them? And how can anyone preach unless they are sent? As it is written: "How beautiful are the feet of those who bring good news!" (vv. 11, 13-15)*

Focusing on whos is rarely our first instinct. In addition to the many distractions that make focusing on anything or anyone difficult, two specific things often prevent us from focusing on others:

1) We are selfish and preoccupied with our own self-interests or self-preservation.
2) We become impatient, annoyed, and even resentful of others (usually because they threaten to keep us from accomplishing our self-focused goals).

Was that too honest this early in the book? I know the truth hurts, but we will not be able to effectively focus on whos until we remove these two obstacles. The best way to deal with both of these barriers is to take these thoughts captive and make them submit to the obedience of Christ (2 Cor. 10:5). This is not as hard as it may seem. It is as simple as refocusing the lens of a microscope by making a slight adjustment with the focusing knob.

First, look intently at the face of Jesus. You will see that He is looking with compassion at the person—the who—you are called to serve in whatever particular assignment the Master has privileged you. You will recognize how this looks because His eyes of loving compassion have been fixed on you many times. With that slight turn of the knob, your focus will then become clear. You will no longer fix your attention on yourself because humility comes naturally in the shadow of Jesus. As you maintain this focus on Jesus, you will become more patient, gentle, and longsuffering with this other person because you are no longer representing yourself or your own goals (Eph. 4:2-3). You have become an agent of God's kindness (Rom. 4:2) and mercy (Rom. 12:1). You will focus on the who because you are focusing on Who (Jesus).

Focusing on whos should be the motivation for whatever we do in ministry. Why we do something is probably more significant than what we do. Colossians 3:23-24 says, *Whatever you do, work at it with all your heart, as working for the Lord, not for human masters, since you know that you will receive an inheritance from the Lord as a reward. It is the Lord Christ you are serving.* But if the driving force of our actions in ministry is not focused on whos (and ultimately Who), the work often becomes an end in itself, a burdensome quest of conducting action after action, without ever achieving an eternal result. And when what replaces who, religion may easily replace relationship.

How many well-intentioned Christians are involved in a ministry of some sort without fully understanding why they are involved? Their motives may be pure. Their service is often admirable—even heroic. But why are they ministering? What may have begun with a sincere focus on meeting the needs of others has turned into a frenetic regimen of activities and events to accomplish an ever-increasing checklist of goals and objectives. In some cases, ministry has become nothing more than the drudgery of a job, or worse yet, misery instead of ministry. When our focus has shifted to a what instead of a who, ministry can feel like rowing a boat against the current to an unreachable destination, then burning out in the process.

But when ministry is connected to whos, we then have a viable reason to *run and not grow weary, [to] walk and not be faint* (Isa. 40:31). We have an ongoing motivation to *not become weary in doing good, for at the proper time we will reap a harvest if we do not give up* (Gal. 6:9).

The harvest we want to reap is never going to be a what.

It will always be a who.

# CHAPTER 2

# One Incredible Day with Jesus

*For there is one God and one mediator*
*between God and mankind,*
*the man Christ Jesus, who gave himself as a ransom for all people.*
1 Timothy 2:5-6

*"Let us go over to the other side,"* Jesus said. This probably was not what His disciples wanted to hear at the end of a long day—actually, a long week. Crowds from all over the region had been pressing in on them since Jesus had arrived at Capernaum on the Sea of Galilee several days before. Everyone had heard about the miracles He was performing—especially the healings. They brought their friends and relatives who were sick and afflicted, hoping they could somehow make their way through the crowds to get close enough for Jesus to touch them and heal them. The disciples grew weary as they tried to keep the crowds from crushing Jesus in the fray.

Jesus had to be exhausted, yet His compassion for people drove Him to minister to them, sometimes without rest or food. And His passion to teach them—feed them—with wisdom and truth through parables about the Kingdom of Heaven was endless. Often He pulled His disciples aside to share with them the deeper meaning of the parables. For the rest of their lives, they cherished those special times of instruction by the Master and shared them with others.

On this particular day, Jesus had instructed His disciples to prepare a boat for Him on the seashore. From its bow, He taught the assembled crowd with less interruption, although other boats often pulled alongside. This memorable day of teaching included one of His most famous parables: the Sower and the Seed. He emphasized that seeds needed to have good soil in order to grow and produce an abundant crop. Seeds would not grow properly on a worn path, in rocky places, or among thorns. They had to be sown in good soil. He explained privately to His disciples that the seed was the Word of God. The good soil represented a person who heard the word, accepted it, and produced a crop—thirty, sixty, or even one hundred times what was sown (Mark 4:20). Despite Jesus' private explanation, the disciples struggled to understand what He meant. Perhaps a field trip would help to illustrate His teaching further.

Near the end of that long day, Jesus said to His disciples, *"Let us go over to the other side"* (Mark 4:35). Imagine the look of astonishment on their faces. Their response in that moment—if not spoken directly to Jesus Himself—was certainly mumbled to one another: "Why would He want us to go to the other side of the Sea of Galilee now? Why not eat supper and get a good night's sleep first? Crossing to the other side could take all night, and we're already exhausted. Besides, there's nothing on that side of the sea except pagan, idol-worshiping Gentiles."

Jews in Jesus' day knew that the other side of the Sea of Galilee was a forbidden place. As young boys, the disciples had all been warned by their parents: "Never go to the other side!" They would only find trouble waiting for them over there. And their parents were correct. The other side was the region of the Decapolis—ten cities established by the famous Roman general Ptolemy, about ninety years before, as an extension of Rome's power and dominance. Located in modern-day Syria, the region was known for its worship of Roman gods and rituals that included the sacrifice of pigs.

But dutifully, and with all the strength they could muster, the disciples followed their Rabbi's instructions and set out to row across the eight miles of dark water, accompanied by several other small boats. Can you hear the creaking of the boat and the slap of the wooden oars against the water with each labored stroke? A profound tiredness must have overcome the disciples by this point—the kind of mind-numbing tiredness and monotony of rowing that causes people to turn things over and over in their mind: "Is this it? Is this what we signed up to do when we answered Jesus' call to come and follow Him? Crowd control? Boat rowing? Why are we doing this? There's nothing on the other side but trouble!"

Amid the tedium of their rowing, these thoughts were violently and suddenly interrupted. *A furious squall came up, and the waves broke over the boat, so that it was nearly swamped* (Mark 4:37).

These veteran fishermen realized quickly that this was no ordinary storm. In fact, it was more like a typhoon and earthquake combined—a *megas* (exceedingly great, high, large, loud, mighty, strong) *seismos* (earthquake).[3] This storm seemed angry and oppressive, as if the boat were the target of evil spiritual forces attempting to prevent Jesus and His disciples from keeping their God-ordained appointment on the other side. As if life were not already hard enough for these worn-out disciples, they also had to survive a life-and-death experience in the dead of night in the middle of the Sea of Galilee.

And to make matters even worse, *Jesus was in the stern, sleeping on a cushion* (Mark 4:38).

How can this be? Something had gone terribly wrong, and suddenly, everything spun out of control for these experienced Galilean fishermen. The wind swirled and waves crashed over the front and sides of the boat. One after another, an endless barrage of brilliant lightning strikes followed by deafening thunderclaps tormented them. They clung to the edge of the boat as it filled with water, then emptied again as the rolling waves tossed it hither and yon. The disciples' fear and anxiety turned to despair.

Then suddenly, in a final act of desperation, the disciples remembered that Jesus was in the boat with them. They rushed to wake Him, crying out to Him in their anguish, *"Don't you care if we drown?"* (Mark 4:38). They did not ask, "Will you help us fight for survival as one of the crew?" Neither did they ask, "Will you perform a miracle and rescue us from this storm?" No. They asked, *"Don't you care?"*

Where was the disciples' faith? That is one of the questions Jesus asked them: *"Why are you so afraid? Do you still have no faith?"* (Mark 4:40). After all, they had seen Jesus perform remarkable miracles. He had cast out demons and healed many sick people, but those seemed like isolated incidents. This was different—a storm at sea—something these fishermen were more qualified to handle than a rabbi was. These veteran fishermen were quite accustomed to the Sea of Galilee and its familiar gale-force winds and waves. They frequented these waters that were six hundred fifty feet lower in elevation than the Mediterranean Sea, only thirty miles away. It was not the first time they had experienced the rapidly descending cool, dry wind hitting the humid air above the sea, producing a violent storm.[4]

But this was definitely different.

They panicked and feared all would be lost.

But at some point in the tumultuous sea, before it seemed the boat would finally break apart, they awakened Jesus. Perhaps they needed Him to help batten down the hatches, furl the sails, take a turn at the oars, or bail water. Scripture does not tell what they thought He might be able to do to help them, but they obviously believed He was ignoring their peril. Jesus did not seem to care that they were about to drown.

The help Jesus provided may have been the last thing any of the disciples could have fathomed—that Jesus could, in an instant, silence the violent winds and waves with only these words: *"Peace, be still"* (Mark 4:39 NKJV). But He did. In that same instant, their fear of the storm transitioned to a fear of the One who could completely control it. They said, *"Who is this? Even the wind and waves obey him!"* (Mark 4:41).

We do not know how long it took to make landfall, but it must have been an interesting segment of the journey. Surreal calm overshadowed them—both of nature and of soul. Only the quiet, rhythmic lapping of water against the wooden hull of the boat and the occasional splash of the oars interrupted the silence. No one dared to speak as they contemplated the mystery of what they had witnessed. But they were only beginning to experience what would become one of the most incredible days of their lives.

The morning light broke across the clear blue sky. Finally, the long night had passed and land was visible on the horizon. Only hours ago, it seemed their lives would end in a watery grave. But now, hope arose with the dawn of a new day—on the other side. Land. Glorious land was visible as the glistening morning sunlight danced across the water. Can you imagine the relief they must have felt when they finally made it safely to shore? Soon they would be warming themselves by a fire on the beach, drying their sea-soaked clothing, and recounting their thoughts about the night they had barely survived. Perhaps they would ask Jesus to explain how he quieted the wind and the waves with three spoken words.

But just as the boat was landing and before anyone could disembark, a wild-eyed, crazy man ran toward the boat, screaming. (Matthew's gospel says there were two men.) Had the disciples survived the worst night of their lives only to be killed by savages on the shore? Surely one of them must have thought, *My parents were right—never go to the other side!*

Without hesitation, Jesus climbed out of the boat to speak with one of the demon-possessed men; perhaps His disciples huddled in the stern, clutching their oars in case they were needed as weapons.

But remember, this was someone's son or brother—maybe he was a husband or father. Scripture does not reveal how he had come to this tragic point in his demon-possessed life—living among the tombs, cutting himself, and crying out in torment through the night, breaking the iron shackles meant to contain his rage. While others saw him through eyes of fear, Jesus saw him through eyes of compassion. The disciples soon realized that Jesus had brought them to the other side of the sea for this man. They had not been going to a destination; they had been going to a person—a who.

In the same way that He had spoken to the storm, Jesus cast out this legion of demons, as many as 6,000 of them—with only His words.[5] He then sent them into the herd of 2,000 sacrificial pigs that ran down the cliff and drowned themselves. Within moments, the man, freed from the demons, was sitting at Jesus' feet, *clothed and in his right mind* (Mark 5:15 ESV). What did Jesus say to the man? What did the man say to Jesus in those private moments—his mind free of the noise and his heart filled with indescribable love? Jesus had come from the other side to rescue him, to save him, and to change the course of his life.

The disciples must have wondered why Jesus had come to rescue this man and why He was spending time with him. He was a Gentile, he was demon-possessed, and he lived on the wrong side of the Sea of Galilee—in the godforsaken Decapolis. What use could Jesus possibly have for this man? Yet they could not deny the surreal calm that overshadowed the new follower of Jesus.

Can you imagine the difference in this man's life? How long had it been since he had experienced a clear thought? When was the last time he had felt no fear? When had he ever felt such freedom? Peace, be still. No wonder the man's first question as a new believer was to ask Jesus if he could get in the boat and follow Him (Mark 5:18). Were the skeptical disciples reluctant to invite him to join them? What if he had a sudden relapse in the boat?

Probably to the disciples' great relief, Jesus told the man that he could not go with them. Instead, Jesus instructed him to go back home to his people and tell them what had happened. *So the man went away and began to tell in the Decapolis how much Jesus had done for him. And all the people were amazed* (Mark 5:20). What a day of rejoicing and celebration it must have been when this lost son, brother, father, or friend came back home a new man.

Jesus' clear focus on this day was simply remarkable. He was not distracted by the storm. He was not troubled by the demons. He never lost sight of His true purpose for this journey.

He focused on a who.

# CHAPTER 3

# A Stunning End to the Incredible Day

*Anyone who belongs to Christ has become a new person.*
*The old life is gone; a new life has begun!*
2 Corinthians 5:17 (NLT)

The field trip for the disciples did not end in the Decapolis. Totally exhausted from the previous night and their encounter with the demon-possessed man (not to mention the angry pig farmers) the next morning, the weary disciples began the long journey back to the other side of the sea. Perhaps they thought they would finally be able to go back to home sweet Capernaum for some much needed rest.

But Jesus had other plans.

As soon as they landed on the other shore, a large crowd swarmed Jesus. They had been waiting for Him. Did the disciples assume Jesus would tell everyone how tired they were and how they needed to rest and recuperate?

They should have known better.

Jesus had not come to be served but to serve others.

Just then, one of the synagogue rulers from Capernaum, Jairus, came and fell at Jesus' feet, pleading with Him to come and heal his dying daughter. She must have been so sick that he could not bring her to Jesus. Perhaps Jairus's faith had been ignited a few days earlier when Jesus cast out an evil spirit from a man in his own synagogue in Capernaum (Mark 1:21-28). Maybe Jairus had recognized Jesus' authority over evil spirits then, and in his final hour of desperation to rescue his daughter, Jesus became his only hope.

Mark simply wrote, *so Jesus went with him* (Mark 5:24).

That is tremendous. In His compassion, Jesus was drawn not only to Jairus's strong faith, but also to the opportunity to demonstrate His own focus in ministry—to restore someone's life.

Can you envision the disciples as they trudged alongside Jesus, trying feebly, and without much success, to shield Him from the pressing crowd? Did their patience wear thin as people in the crowd pushed against them, desperately trying to get close enough to touch Jesus, hoping for a miracle of their own? The fact that Jairus had already managed to get through their perimeter and had grasped Jesus by His feet seemed like a failure on the disciples' part—especially since Jesus agreed to go to Jairus's house. Others cried out in the streets, *"Son of David, have mercy on us!"* (Matt. 9:27 NLT).

He did.

He always did.

The disciples must have been so fatigued—every step feeling more arduous than the last as they walked toward Capernaum. Perhaps they attempted to form a human barricade around Jesus to keep the people from crushing Him as everyone tried to see or receive a miracle. In that moment, Jesus turned around in the crowd and asked what seemed like a ridiculous question:*"Who touched my clothes?"* (Mark 5:30).

His disciples did not even try to hide their frustration at this point. Their curt response provides a glimpse into their physical and mental disposition: *"You see the people crowding against you ... and yet you can ask, 'Who touched me?'"* (v. 31). If someone had broken through to touch Jesus, it was only further proof of their inability to protect Him from the crowd. Were they thinking that this job of crowd control was about as rewarding as boat rowing to godforsaken places and back?

The answer to Jesus' question eventually was provided by a most pitiful woman, exposed within the crowd as she tried to slink away. She should not have been there. Because of the Jewish laws for women who were bleeding, she was not allowed to be out in public—or actually to be in contact with anyone. She was considered unclean. After twelve years of exhausting every financial and human resource available, she had not been able to stop the bleeding. Can you imagine how lonely this woman must have been—without human contact for twelve years? Yet, in her desperation, she thought if she could only somehow sneak through the crowd unnoticed and touch the hem of Jesus' garment, she would be healed.

What faith! What courage! What risk of public humiliation and possible punishment for contaminating everyone else in the process of trying to secure for herself the healing she had sought for many years.

But it worked. Somehow she managed to reach Him without being seen, and she instantly felt the healing in her body when she touched His garment. But she was not the only one who noticed. Jesus felt the healing power leave His body, and he was not willing to allow her to disappear without receiving the full extent of her miracle. This woman became the focus of His full attention.

"It happened in the middle of a crowd; but the crowd was forgotten and Jesus spoke to that woman as if she was the only person in the world. She was a poor, unimportant sufferer, with a trouble that made her unclean, and yet to that one unimportant person Jesus gave all of Himself."[6] He said to her, *"Daughter, your faith has healed you. Go in peace and be freed from your suffering"* (Mark 5:34). "In those fifteen little words Jesus had given her restoration, acceptance, affection, belonging, *love*. And He did it *publicly*."[7] Her faith had brought her healing and now she could go in peace, free from her suffering. Once again, Jesus had spoken, *"Peace, be still."*

In the commotion surrounding this out-of-place woman, others had pressed through the crowd as well. They were messengers from Jairus's house with the terrible news that his daughter had died. *"Why bother the teacher anymore?"* they asked (Mark 5:35).

Jesus ignored them.

Wow!

Do not miss this important fact, which Mark includes in the narrative (Mark 5:36). Jesus ignored them because he was focused intently on rescuing that little girl. In that moment, he reminded Jairus, *"Don't be afraid; just believe"* (v. 36).

Jesus demonstrated an incredible ability to focus simultaneously on the woman who was bleeding, Jairus, and Jairus's daughter. He was ready to meet all their needs and ultimately give them abundant life (John 10:10). Jesus could have easily become distracted by the woman's uncleanness,

Jairus's messengers delivering bad news, or by the disciples' less than encouraging attitudes, but He remained solely focused on those He came to serve—the whos.

The scene at Jairus's house was disconcerting. The death of a child is devastating, but even more disappointing because Jesus had been coming to heal her. Surely the disciples had heard Him tell Jairus to not be afraid— just believe. Did it remind them of Jesus' words to them the previous night in the storm when they were near death? As they approached the house and heard the people crying and wailing loudly, were they shocked to hear Jesus' statement: *"The child is not dead, but asleep"* (Mark 5:39)? How could He know that? What went through the minds of the disciples when the mourners laughed at Jesus' words of faith? Were they embarrassed, or did they believe along with Jairus? At this point, only Peter, James, John, Jairus, and his wife were invited by Jesus to go in where the child was lying.

Jesus said, *"Talitha koum!"* Mark records the Aramaic transliteration for *"Little girl, I say to you, get up!"* (Mark 5:41). With those words, Jairus's twelve-year-old daughter rose from the dead. What overwhelming joy must have filled that awestruck room of eyewitnesses to a miracle of miracles! Once again, instantaneously, peace was restored to Jairus's home. Peace, be still.

What a stunning end to this incredible 24-hour day. Jesus' perfect peace had rescued the perishing, repaired the destroyed, restored the distressed, and resurrected the dead. And He was not finished. Matthew tells us that immediately after Jesus left Jairus's house, He healed two blind men who called out to Him for mercy, and He cast out an evil spirit who was causing a man to be mute (Matt. 9:27-32).

Indeed, Jesus' lesson about the seed falling on good soil and producing an abundant crop had been clearly illustrated for His disciples: the good soil in His focus is always a who.

# CHAPTER 4

# Follow the Eyes of Jesus

*I will instruct you and teach you in the way you should go;*
*I will guide you with My eye.*
Psalm 32:8 (NKJV)

As I reflect on the disciples' incredible experience with Jesus, I have tried to follow the eyes of Jesus throughout the narrative. In the midst of the furious storm that nearly swamped the boat, can you see Jesus' eyes focused intently on His disciples? He saw their fear and lack of faith as their circumstances overwhelmed them. His eyes were filled with compassion as He realized they did not know what to do. He cared deeply for them, so He quieted the wind and waves on their behalf.

Do you see the eyes of Jesus looking with pity on the wretched, demon-possessed man? When was the last time this man had seen anyone look at him that way? He had only seen fear, anger, and hate in the eyes of those who had dared to look at him. But can you see the merciful and loving eyes of Jesus looking down at the man who kneeled before Him? As Jesus had acted on the disciples' behalf to calm the storm, He acted on the demon-possessed man's behalf to set him free from his horrifying condition. Can you also see the confidence in Jesus' eyes as He commissioned this new missionary to go and share the good news with others? When was the last time anyone had believed in this man's ability to do anything worthy of recognition? But Jesus did.

Do you see Jesus' eyes as He listened attentively to Jairus's earnest pleas for his little girl? Even with the rush of the crowd and the mental and physical exhaustion Jesus must have been experiencing, He stopped everything else He was doing to focus on Jairus. Jesus then acted immediately to meet his need. Can you see Jesus' reassuring look when His eyes met Jairus's eyes as they walked toward his house after the news about his daughter had been delivered? Jairus's eyes communicated exactly what Jesus had said, *"Don't be afraid; just believe."*

And while they were walking, can you see Jesus' eyes when He stopped and scanned the crowd looking for the recipient of His healing power? He searched for her—the woman who was hiding in fear of being found out. Can you imagine what she must have felt when His eyes met hers? What compassion! What unconditional love and acceptance! When was the last time she had seen anyone look at her with anything other than disgust? But His gaze was one of restoration and freedom, for His eyes were filled with unconditional love.

And what about Jairus's daughter? What did she see in the eyes of her Life-giver when she opened her once lifeless eyes? She *beheld his glory—the glory as of the only begotten of the Father, full of grace and truth. In him was life, and the life was the light of men and the light shines in the darkness…* and His life brought her life (John 1:14 NKJV).

If we follow the eyes of Jesus on that day, we realize that they are always focused on people—the whos. In their despair, their hopelessness, and their darkest hour, Jesus sees them and takes action. He rescues and restores them, making it possible for them to reach their full potential. While the storm blows around Him, while demons rage, and while naysayers dismiss Him, He never removes His focus from those who need His mercy.

Consider the words of Zephaniah 3:17:

> *For the LORD your God is living among you.*
> *He is a mighty savior.*
> *He will take delight in you with gladness.*
> *With his love, he will calm all your fears.*
> *He will rejoice over you with joyful songs.* (NLT)

While it may be encouraging to follow the eyes of Jesus on this particular day, it is not so encouraging to follow His disciples' eyes. While Jesus remained steadily focused on whos, they only focused on whats. In the boat, their eyes are fixed firmly on the storm and their self-preservation. That is somewhat understandable because they had to row the boat to the destination Jesus had given them. But in their despair, they forgot one significant thing—Jesus was *in* the boat with them. Had they taken a moment to control their emotions and replace their fear with faith, they could have asked Him what they should do. Instead, in their pride and self-sufficiency, they incorrectly judged that Jesus did not care about them or their condition. They focused on themselves and on their circumstances.

We understand the disciples' response to the demon-possessed man. To say it was terrifying is probably putting it mildly. It is not so much what the disciples actually did, but what they did not do. They did not even get out of the boat. But Jesus did. Was it because the disciples were afraid? Actually, they also were afraid of Jesus after He had calmed the storm. Maybe they were frozen in fear. Or maybe they did not see any reason to come to this region of the Decapolis, where pagan Gentiles lived, sacrificing their pigs to Roman gods among other things too disgusting to mention.[8] So once again, the disciples' eyes were fixed on themselves and their circumstances—out of fear, apathy, or both.

Do you become more sympathetic toward the disciples the longer the day becomes? I do. We know what it is like to be awake all night battling some kind of overwhelming, catastrophic difficulty. It saps all our energy. Add to this, the fact that they had rowed back and forth across the eight miles on the sea.

Exhausting.

Crowd control on the shore was definitely not something they wanted to do either. It likely tried their weary souls. I often become impatient and irritated when I am tired. Nevertheless, when I try to see the disciples' eyes at this point, they seem to have lost sight of why they are following Jesus. Their sarcastic response when Jesus asked who touched Him provides some insight into their state of mind. If they had been paying close attention throughout the day, they would have realized that whenever Jesus had an encounter with someone, that person's life was about to change. Once again, the disciples' focus is on what (crowd control) versus who, namely the woman who was healed by touching Jesus' robe. They also may have been upset with her since she was diseased and her presence in the crowd made everyone unclean.

Finally, when the messengers from Jairus's house arrived with news of his daughter's death, on what were the disciples' eyes focused? Were they fixed on Jesus and His response to Jairus? Did the disciples reassure Jairus with their confident looks? Or were their eyes more in alignment with the messengers who stated what the disciples might have thought: do not bother Jesus (or us) anymore. Again, their focus is on what instead of who.

Could it be that we are no different from the disciples in our ministry alongside Jesus? While His focus is constantly on the whos around us, our focus drifts toward the whats that consume our time and energy. Are we exhausted from trying to survive the storms we battle? Are we hiding from the attacks the enemy launches in our direction? Have we given up on people and situations that seem impossible? Have we resorted to mindless boat rowing and busy crowd control?

What would happen if we stopped long enough to look up from our struggle at the oars and from our compassionless ministries to catch one glimpse of Jesus' eyes?

Would His eyes be focused on whats or on whos?

## CHAPTER 5

# Rowing to the Other Side Ministries

*For the wisdom of this world is foolishness to God.*
1 Corinthians 3:19 (NLT)

The following scenario is hypothetical. It does not take place in the Bible. But I wonder if it may take place in some of our Christian ministries today.

It was another day of strategic planning for key leadership members at Upper Room headquarters in Jerusalem. Almost thirty years had passed since Jesus had commissioned them to go and make disciples of all nations. At first, things had gone well, especially in Jerusalem, where the apostles, often empowered to perform miracles, had been able to preach the good news of the resurrection of Jesus Christ. Sure, there was opposition. That was to be expected. Jesus Himself had been beaten and crucified for teaching the truth.

The leadership also had been greatly encouraged when Saul of Tarsus had become a believer. He, along with Barnabas, had already taken the gospel to Gentiles beyond Judea. Churches had been established throughout the Roman Empire. Encouraging reports from multiple underground churches, despite severe persecution, had come from Rome itself.

Now the key leaders from throughout the region gathered to meet with the apostles and plan the next phase of growth and development to fulfill the Great Commission of Jesus Christ. After studying all the statistical reports and considering the strengths, weaknesses, opportunities, and obstacles, the leadership needed strategic initiatives and strategies for the next five years. The floor was open for discussion.

"I think we should consider launching a new initiative here in Jerusalem to strengthen our base," said James, the moderator. "We could start an additional fundraising program to feed the poor. I suggest we purchase some property and establish a Christian university for Great Commission Studies."

A buzz of conversation filled the room. A Christian university seemed like a good idea, but with all the persecution Christians were experiencing, perhaps another city would be better suited for that project. Barnabas suggested Antioch since a strong church movement existed there. Others contested something that important should remain in Jerusalem to ensure doctrinal purity was maintained. Still others advocated that Corinth might be a suitable location given its strong donor base.

While this initiative was still being discussed and debated, John stood and offered a different approach: "Maybe we should ask, what was Jesus' model of ministry? What was His most successful strategy for reaching people with the gospel?"

The room stirred with support. Spurred by their encouragement, John continued. "Instead of putting all our energy into something that has never been done, maybe we should go back and revisit the fundamentals."

Luke agreed enthusiastically. "Remember the time Jesus fed the 5,000? That was a real crowd-pleaser. If we could put together a large-scale feeding program, we could draw giant crowds and share the gospel with them."

Almost immediately, Thomas argued, "But where will we get all the food? Jesus multiplied the fish and the loaves, but unless that happened at each gathering, feeding large crowds would cost a fortune."

John said, "How about the time Jesus attended the Feast of Tabernacles? Many people believed on Him there. Maybe we should plan an annual rally during this feast when everyone is already gathering for the upcoming Passover."

That idea gained momentum among those in attendance.

"Yes!" Peter interjected. "That was a turning point in the minds of people about Jesus being the promised Messiah."

Excitedly, others joined the conversation, offering their ideas to boost attendance at such a rally. Their suggestions included things such as launching a promotional campaign, providing live entertainment, and hosting a parade, which would begin at the Mount of Olives and retrace Jesus' triumphant entry into Jerusalem, complete with palm branches and a riderless donkey!

James interrupted the cacophony of increasingly diverse suggestions and opinions. "Gentlemen, gentlemen," he said, "we have generated three excellent ideas to consider: a Christian university for Great Commission Studies, a large-scale food distribution program that would attract crowds, and an annual rally during the Feast of Tabernacles. These all have merit, but we haven't heard from our Gentile brothers from regions beyond Jerusalem. What do you suggest, Timothy?"

Timothy pastored the church at Ephesus. He and the other Gentile leaders who accompanied him had traveled great distances to attend the meeting. After expressing gratitude to James for including the Gentile leadership, he responded, "It isn't enough to hold large-scale gatherings every year here in Jerusalem. We need to take the gospel to the ends of the world. Many regions beyond ours haven't heard the name of Jesus."

"But how can we extend our reach that far?" James asked.

Peter jumped to his feet and said, "Remember when Jesus told us to take Him in a boat to the other side of the Sea of Galilee? We almost died in a terrible storm before landing in the region of the Decapolis, a place filled with Gentiles. Later, when we returned there, we discovered that the good news about Jesus had become known throughout the region. I've even heard that some of the believers from that area have taken the gospel back with them to Rome itself. Should we focus our attention on rowing to the other side of the Sea of Galilee?"

Chatter grew louder and louder. Peter's idea resonated with Jewish and Gentile leaders alike. It was consistent with the original notion of doing something after the model of Jesus' ministry. It also had Great Commission written all over it. Consensus grew, and soon the room bustled with small groups working by committee to map out particular strategic initiatives to propel the suggestion forward. One committee was assigned the task of generating a name for this new initiative. Another committee was busy determining the necessary resources for such a worthy endeavor. Still another worked through various promotional aspects to ensure that support was achievable by all represented churches.

The enthusiasm grew. "Let's call it Rowing to the Other Side Ministries," suggested one of the naming committee members.

"Are you sure?" challenged someone else. "An organization called Staying on This Side Ministries is headquartered in Capernaum. We wouldn't want anyone to confuse us with that group."

"I think the name is different enough to prevent any confusion," the naming committee member urged.

Hearing no further opposition, James took his quill and wrote Rowing to the Other Side Ministries at the top of the parchment. "It's official," he said. "Resources Committee? What have you come up with for us to consider?"

"Well, obviously we'll need to secure a boat," said Matthias, the subcommittee chairman. "We can't possibly go to the other side without a boat."

Muffled laughter echoed through the room along with a whispered joke from someone about how hard it would be to swim to the other side.

"Well, it's true," said Matthias, with more seriousness in his voice. "Are any of you still connected with the fishing industry near the Sea of Galilee?"

James said, "I still have a few contacts in the area. But I don't think one boat is going to be enough. If Rowing to the Other Side Ministries is going to be effective, we'll need to launch a fleet of boats."

Multiple responses reverberated through the room.

"How many boats are you suggesting?" asked Peter.

James replied, "We won't be taken seriously if we have less than five boats."

"Why stop with five?" asked Peter. "We should start with twelve—one named for each of the tribes of Israel. Or maybe we should name them after the twelve apostles."

Chuckles rippled through the room.

"Wait a minute!" Timothy interrupted. "I think we're going about this the wrong way. We need to back up and think more strategically. Why don't we construct a boat-building factory near the Sea of Galilee? Then we can build all the boats we want to build."

"Hear, hear!" said several others.

A boat-building factory was something everyone could get excited about. It would ensure not only an immediate launch of a strong Great Commission effort, but also it would ensure the perpetuation of the ministry for many years to come. The boats could be manufactured, maintained, and repaired. Committees reassembled to consider everything necessary to launch this new ministry complete with its own boat-building factory.

Only one small problem emerged from the feverish planning. Where would Rowing to the Other Side Ministries find enough capable sailors with the rowing skills necessary to constantly cross the Sea of Galilee? The answer was almost too easy. On the same property where the boat-building factory was to be built, a companion ministry would be started simultaneously: Other Side School of Rowing, staffed with the finest rowing instructors and the latest in nautical technology. A specialized technical aspect of the school would be its state-of-the-art woodworking shop where each student would construct a custom-made set of oars. The sons of fishermen for miles around would, no doubt, stand in line to gain admission to this institution of higher rowing.

As soon as the meeting adjourned, everyone set out to build the ministries. Less than one year later, everything was ready for the ribbon-cutting ceremony for Rowing to the Other Side Ministries (ROSM) and its academy, Other Side School of Rowing (OSSR). As anticipated, a crowd gathered on the hillside to watch as three dozen boats were put into the water, ready to embark on their maiden voyage to the other side of the Sea of Galilee. Music played as the parade of academy graduates marched toward their new boats, each one with his own set of custom oars displayed at shoulder arms. Mothers and fathers pointed out their sailors while younger boys imitated the graduates with their own self-crafted oars made of sticks and driftwood. The leaders gathered near the shore to oversee the official launch.

With a sudden synchronized splash, the vision of Rowing to the Other Side Ministries became a reality. To everyone's surprise, as soon as the first thirty-six boats pulled away from the shore, the next thirty-six were brought out of the factory and placed into the water. A cheer erupted from the crowd as another group of academy graduates marched toward the new boats.

"This is unbelievable!" said one of the bystanders. "It's so good to see the Great Commission of Jesus taking place right before our very eyes."

Then another splash occurred, followed by another fleet of boats, followed by another team of boat rowers. The first boats were nearly out of sight, their sailors rowing with all their might so as not to be overtaken by the subsequent waves of boats being launched behind them. It appeared that an effective ministry had been successfully launched.

In the months and years that followed, ROSM launched hundreds of boats equipped with their much-acclaimed fleet of specially trained oarsmen. They frenetically raced back and forth and back and forth and back and forth across the Sea of Galilee. One boat-building factory soon became two; the two then became a franchise with establishments on other large bodies of water. ROSM actually won awards from the local fishing communities. Its school of rowing, also franchised, was recognized by one of the most prominent Greek universities in the region.  Success!

But success comes with a price. From all outward appearances, the ministry seemed to be thriving—always growing, always launching new factories, and always visible with large fleets of boats churning back and forth across the water. However, the debt incurred for the construction of the new factories was mounting and donations were diminishing. Enrollment in the rowing schools was also a challenge. Fewer young men seemed interested in rowing, or maybe it was the number of rowing schools that competed for students. Either way, the financial challenges became an increasing burden.

The factory workers and sailors were reportedly growing weary of their intense labor and long hours. Their leaders reminded them of their worthy purpose: they served in the fulfillment of the Great Commission of Jesus Christ. Effective ministry often comes from great sacrifice, so they needed to press toward the mark of their high calling and consider it a privilege to participate in such a ministry.

But the workers' joy continued to evaporate. Laboring at the oars day after day was tiresome. The harder they worked, the more their service seemed like a job—routine and monotonous. Gone was the excitement of joining ROSM or the OSSR. Their talk of accomplishing the Great Commission of Jesus Christ was gradually replaced with frustrated conversations about the tedium of operating deadlines and the growing lists of expectations.

Soon, the number one priority for Rowing to the Other Side Ministries and its Academy, Other Side School of Rowing, changed: "exist to exist" became the prevailing motivation.

What is wrong with this story? The vision seemed strong: fulfill the Great Commission of Jesus Christ. The mission seemed noteworthy: follow in the model of Jesus' ministry. The method also seemed strategically valid: reach the nations with the gospel by multiplying the outreach efforts. But amid all its apparent success, something does not seem right. What is it?

The story has no who.

ROSM and OSSR are completely dedicated to what.

This is the sad reality of many Christian ministries. Perhaps they began with a clear focus on the whos—reach the lost, minister to the needy, or educate students from a biblical perspective. But somewhere along the way, the focus gradually shifted away from whos to whats. It is a subtle shift—one that first occurs out of necessity, then becomes a competing focus. Soon, the tyranny of the whats replaces the urgency of the whos. While it is true that certain resources (whats) are needed for effective ministry, leaders must ensure they do not become an end in themselves.

Consider Jesus' approach to going to the other side. He was clearly focused on the whos. He was going to rescue the demon-possessed man and launch him into an evangelistic ministry in the Decapolis. For Jesus to be effective in reaching this man, He required a specific resource—a boat. A what. And, as it turned out, it was a significant what. Initially, the boat shielded Him from the pressing crowd and enabled Him to teach eternal truth about the Kingdom of God. Then the same boat was used to transport Him to the other side of the Sea of Galilee, providing a place of refuge for Him and His disciples from the demon-incited storm intended to kill all of them. Notice that Jesus did not take His need for a boat lightly. In fact, two days before their journey to other side, He sent His disciples to the Sea of Galilee to secure a boat for Him to use (Mark 3:9). So, we can learn from Jesus' ministry model that a proper focus on whos often relies on the strategic use of whats.

But what happens when we get these two reversed? What happens when our focus becomes consumed with the whats of ministry to the point that the whos are overshadowed or forgotten in the process? Can we become addicted to building the ministry organization itself along with all its resources to ensure it will continue to exist? If so, for what purpose? And for whom?

How much of our ministry feels like endless boat building and rowing classes? Sure, our drive may have initially come from an eager motivation to do what Jesus said: *"Let us go over to the other side."* And we want to accomplish what He has asked us to do. But the real question should be, is Jesus in the boat at all? Without Him, all our rowing and accomplishing is in vain, even if it is done in His name. In the end, ministry becomes a flurry of activity that produces more and more what and not a single who.

Jesus is not in focus.

People are not in focus.

Boat building and rowing are in focus.

This is religion without relationship.

This is what, not who.

# CHAPTER 6

# Blurry Focus

*And they came to Bethsaida. And some people brought to him
a blind man and begged him to touch him. And he took the
blind man by the hand and led him out of the village, and
when he had spit on his eyes and laid his hands on him, he
asked him, "Do you see anything?" And he looked up and
said, "I see people, but they look like trees, walking." Then
Jesus laid his hands on his eyes again; and he opened his
eyes, his sight was restored, and he saw everything clearly.*
Mark 8:22-25 (ESV)

This miracle is unique—the only two-stage miracle Jesus performed.
Obviously, He could have simply healed this blind man instantly, but He
was illustrating something important for His disciples: it is possible to see
and yet not see clearly.

Only moments before, the disciples were bemoaning the fact that they
had not brought along enough bread for their journey. Keep in mind this
was immediately after Jesus had fed more than 4,000 people by miraculously
multiplying bread and fish. Jesus had reproved the disciples and asked, "*Do
you have eyes but fail to see?*" (Mark 8:18). They had seen the miracle with
their own eyes and had participated in it with their own hands, yet they
had failed to see clearly the significance of Who performed it.

Nothing is worse than blurry focus. It can be as simple as having
smudge marks on a pair of eyeglasses to viewing something through a

telescope that is out of focus. Something is not right. We see the image, but it is hazy, unclear, and indistinct. In certain activities where precision is required, this kind of blurriness can cause a costly miscalculation or error. For those of us involved in the ministry of Christian education, blurry focus might make the difference in whether or not a student grows spiritually while entrusted to our care.

A number of sources contribute to blurry focus in ministry. Sin, selfishness, and self-reliance come to mind. These occur when we allow a wrong focus to compete with the right one. We take our eyes off Jesus and off the people He has called us to serve, and we become preoccupied with ourselves. Other sources of blurry focus include worry, distractions, and weariness. These occur when we allow fear to replace faith, gradually damaging our focus.

# Sin Causes Blurry Focus

*Don't get sidetracked; keep your feet from*
*following evil.* Proverbs 4:27 (NLT)

"Get up! We need to have our quiet time."

Those words sounded odd to me when my new friend, Jonathan, first spoke them. When I looked at my watch and saw that it was 4:30 a.m., all I could think of was, *I was having a quiet time until you woke me up!* But Jonathan was persuasive; besides he outranked me, so I had no choice but to get up and stagger down the stairway behind him to the laundry room in our barracks to pray and read the Bible with him. I had given my life to Jesus Christ two days earlier—the result of the evangelistic outreach of the Navigators[9] on my United States Marine Corps base. Jonathan was assigned to disciple me. He was 100 percent Marine and 100 percent Christian, so essential things such as having a morning quiet time (devotions), memorizing Bible verses, and attending weekly Bible studies became a requirement for me. I am grateful those spiritual disciplines were forged into my Christian life through two years of Navigator discipleship.

Jonathan was serious about his Christian faith, and he was sacrificially diligent about mentoring me—almost on a daily basis—although he was stationed in a different unit on our base. After three months, I was growing strong spiritually through quality time spent in God's Word and prayer. What a blessing to have a brother in Christ to walk alongside me, helping me grow as a Christian believer surrounded by the evils of the world.

Sadly, Jonathan made a terrible decision that caused him to abandon his faith in Christ. While on a deployment, he met a young lady, fell in love with her, and agreed to convert to another religion in order to meet her family's conditions to marry her. As you might imagine, this news crushed me; it shook my faith down to its foundation. How could my mentor in Christianity walk away from everything he believed? Another Navigator Christian (who, by God's grace, discipled me for the next two years) reminded me that King Solomon had done the same thing. It was a difficult experience I have faced several times in my life: other Christians may disappoint me by choosing to *"[love] this present world"* more than Jesus Christ (2 Tim. 4:10 NKJV). This kind of thing happens when we allow sin to remain concealed in our lives. Hidden sin waits for an opportunity to take advantage of us.

Hebrews 12:1 reminds us to *strip off every weight that slows us down, especially the sin that so easily trips us up* (NLT). A popular bumper sticker says, "Christians aren't perfect—just forgiven." This is true, but we can still end up with many scars or even with a shipwrecked faith from being swamped by sin (1 Tim. 1:19). Living an effective Christian life of service is impossible when we are entangled with sin. We need to strip off the weight of sin, as it is an unnecessary encumbrance in the race that has been set before us. I lost contact with Jonathan not long after his decision, but I pray that one day he will return to his first love (Rev. 2:4).

Sin is actually misdirected focus. It causes us to redirect our attention— we shift our gaze away from the holiness of Jesus and His perfect agenda for the eternal work of the Kingdom of God, and instead we focus on the selfish *lust of the flesh, the lust of the eyes, and the pride of life* (1 John 2:16).

> *Don't love the world's ways. Don't love the world's goods. Love of the world squeezes out love for the Father. Practically everything that goes on in the world—wanting your own way, wanting everything for yourself, wanting to appear important—has nothing to do with the Father. It just isolates you from him. The world and all its wanting, wanting, wanting is on the way out—but whoever does what God wants is set for eternity.* (1 John 2:15-17 MSG)

Sin will always be a contender for our focus in Christian ministry. It is an obstacle or trip hazard in the race. Can you imagine how difficult it would be to run a marathon with people trying to trip you along the way? That is exactly what we face. Our enemy wants to trip us to keep us from being effective in accomplishing what God has called us to do. *Stay alert! Watch out for your great enemy, the devil. He prowls around like a roaring lion, looking for someone to devour* (1 Peter 5:8 NLT).

While many sins can trip us in our personal walk with Christ and in our Christian ministry, two are commonly associated with blurry focus: gossip and lust. Interestingly, both are considered secret sins since they are not usually revealed publicly (although social media often exposes them). Both are typically rationalized in the minds of those who commit them— sometimes to the point where people do not even identify these acts as sins. Gossip and lust cause Christians to lose their focus in ministry because they can actually destroy other people, for whom Christ died. If we glance at Jesus' eyes to see how He views the people who are the objects of our gossip or lust, we realize how our focus has been misdirected.

Sadly, some believers (even those serving in Christian ministry) allow sin to remain embedded in their lives. Many times this occurs because they rationalize the sin, or they assume they can do nothing about it other than to seek forgiveness when it happens again and again. This strips away their spiritual victory in life and erodes their confidence in ministry. Some Christians make 1 John 1:9 their life verse: *If we confess our sins, he is faithful and just and will forgive us our sins and purify us from all unrighteousness.* This is a comforting verse for every believer. Jesus is faithful to forgive us when we confess our sins to Him. But do not miss the second part of the verse: He wants to *purify us from all unrighteousness.*

In this passage, the apostle John is talking about walking in the light in righteous fellowship with God and others, purified by the precious blood of Jesus. God wants us to confess our sins so He can make our lives clean. But if this verse is only used as a get-out-of-jail-free pass, believers will continue to be tripped by the same sins, which will rob them of a victorious Christian life and ministry.

I once confronted a Christian man who was openly committing adultery with a woman while his wife was pregnant. Instead of being broken and repentant over his sin, he confidently quoted 1 John 1:9 and said God understood that he had needs his wife could not meet. That is an extreme misuse of this Bible verse, but I wonder how many Christians take a similar approach with their sins, frivolously abusing the grace of God to gratify their selfish desires. This may be why some in Christian ministry have such blurry vision.

Not everyone takes such a flippant approach to sin and God's forgiveness. Many Christians have told me they feel defeated by sin, although they continually try to overcome it with humble repentance.

Romans 6:11-14 is instructive for Christians who feel constantly defeated by sin:

> *In the same way, count yourselves dead to sin but alive to God in Christ Jesus. Therefore do not let sin reign in your mortal body so that you obey its evil desires. Do not offer any part of yourself to sin as an instrument of wickedness, but rather offer yourselves to God as those who have been brought from death to life; and offer every part of yourself to him as an instrument of righteousness. For sin shall no longer be your master, because you are not under the law, but under grace.*

Sin is no longer our master; therefore, we can confidently use our bodies as instruments of righteousness in God's service without permitting sin to control our lives. While we will certainly be tempted to sin, we know that God will provide a way for us to escape as we put our trust in Him (1 Cor. 10:13). When we are free from the control of sin, we can experience deeper fellowship with God, more fully carry out His purpose for our lives, and produce righteousness in our relationships.

Do you remember God's warning to Cain after he had brought the wrong offering? God told him, *"Sin is crouching at the door, eager to control you. But you must subdue it and be its master"* (Gen. 4:7 NLT). Sadly, Cain did not heed God's warning. He murdered his brother, thus ruining his life and his family's life. By God's grace and with the help of the Holy Spirit, our experience can be different. Paul reminds us:

> *But you are not controlled by your sinful nature. You are controlled by the Spirit if you have the Spirit of God living in you…. And Christ lives within you, so even though your body will die because of sin, the Spirit gives you life because you have been made right with God. The Spirit of God, who raised Jesus from the dead, lives in you.* (Rom. 8:9-11 NLT)

Blurry focus often keeps us from experiencing our full capability to live a victorious Christian life and serve others with spiritual assurance, enabling them to *keep in step with the Spirit* (Gal. 5:25). Many Christians are so defeated by sin and guilt in their lives that they lack the confidence to encourage others to grow spiritually. Like the blind man in Mark 8, we need to allow Jesus to heal us completely of our sin and its devastating consequences, enabling us to see Him clearly in focus. Robertson McQuilken reminds us of the amazing privilege we have to experience the victory that comes through our relationship in Christ:

> The most wonderful Person in all the universe offers us more than doctrinal truth, more than exciting experiences; He offers us Himself in an intimate relationship that can be described adequately only as full. And when we respond to Him in uncomplicated—and unreserved—faith, the blessed Holy Spirit gives us, with Himself, truth that we may know all He intends us to know, fruit that we may be all He designed us to be, and gifts that we may do all He purposed for us to do.[10]

## Selfishness Causes Blurry Focus

> *Do nothing from selfishness or empty conceit, but*
> *with humility of mind regard one another as more*
> *important than yourselves.* Philippians 2:3 (NASB)

Selfishness is one of the easiest ways to allow our focus in ministry to become blurry. When Paul wanted to encourage the believers in the church at Philippi, he mentioned that he did not have many people he could send to them because *everyone looks out for their own interests, not those of Jesus Christ* (Phil. 2:21). Thankfully, he was able to send Epaphroditus to provide needed encouragement. Paul described this man as a brother, fellow worker, fellow soldier, messenger, and faithful minister (Phil. 2:25). Epaphroditus was someone that knew how to focus on the whos, not the whats. Apparently, individuals like him were rare in Paul's day, and they probably are rare in our day as well.

Why are we so inclined toward selfishness, even as servants of the Lord in Christian ministry? Maybe we are oriented toward meeting our needs first, which causes us to focus our attention on ourselves. There is some legitimacy in ensuring our needs are met in order to be in a position to meet the needs of others. For example, in the pre-flight safety briefing on an airplane, passengers are always instructed to put on their own oxygen mask before trying to assist others in the event of an emergency. But, if we remain fixated on our needs, we may miss the fact that others around us need our attention and service.

This can happen to us even when we are serving others. We can become so distracted by our priorities in ministry that we gradually shift our focus away from others and onto ourselves. Do you remember what happened during one of Jesus' visits at the home of Martha in Bethany?

> *As Jesus and his disciples were on their way, he came to a*
> *village where a woman named Martha opened her home*
> *to him. She had a sister called Mary, who sat at the Lord's*
> *feet listening to what He said. But Martha was distracted by*
> *all the preparations that had to be made. She came to him*

*and asked, "Lord, don't you care that my sister has left me to do the work by myself? Tell her to help me!"*

*"Martha, Martha," the Lord answered, "you are worried and upset about many things, but few things are needed—or indeed only one. Mary has chosen what is better, and it will not be taken away from her."* (Luke 10:38-42)

Does this kind of thing happen in our Christian schools? Of course. How often do we become like Martha in our service to the Lord, *distracted by all the preparations* and *worried and upset about many things*? Joanna Weaver captures this well:

We miss so much when we insist on being flesh-driven rather than Spirit-led. When we power walk in a Martha spirit—pushing, striving, and conniving—rather than adopting a Mary spirit that says, "Wherever you lead me, Lord, I just want to be close to you," we miss out on so many of God's good ideas... and our chance to be part of them.[11]

Even as we serve Jesus and others in our Christian schools, it is easy to shift our focus to ourselves. In times like these, we may interject our feelings of frustration with others, a sense of injustice or unfairness, and a complaining spirit like Martha did. We can develop a sense of entitlement—a need to be recognized for our efforts—and an expectation for others to join us in our work. In so doing, we redefine ministry as something more like *me-istry*, and we hold others accountable for their failure to accomplish our agenda. This me-focus in ministry was exactly what Jesus rebuked in the religious leaders of His day.

Can we admit it? We are all selfish. And it is hard to separate selfishness from our service. At this dinner, Martha was preparing a meal for a large group of hungry men. No wonder she was worried and distracted—she needed Mary's help in the kitchen. Martha certainly does not seem selfish. After all, she is serving Jesus and His disciples. Of course, we cannot fully know Martha's motives, but listen to her question to Jesus: *"Don't you care that my sister has left me to do all the work by myself?"* That question sounds like the one the disciples asked when they woke Jesus in the storm and asked, *"Don't you care if we drown?"* (Mark 4:38). Martha's ministry to Jesus and others seems to contain a tinge of me-istry. This kind of service has an expectation attached to it: Care about me! Serve me!

How did Martha respond to Jesus when He told her that Mary had chosen the better thing? Did she sit down beside her sister and listen to Jesus? Luke did not mention that she did. Would he not have included something that significant? Perhaps Martha continued her work—disappointed, frustrated, or both. But what could have happened if Martha had joined her sister? Do we ever miss opportunities like that because we are so busy serving the Lord?

Before we criticize Martha, however, we Christian school educators should look into the mirror of this story to see if we can find ourselves there. Do we serve others with an expectation to be recognized, assisted, affirmed, admired, or even served ourselves? Is it possible that while we say we serve others in ministry, we are actually managers in disguise, demanding the service of others? Do people in our ministries feel served, or do they feel managed? Alan Johnson says,

> Man is infected with rebellion against his Creator, and this rebellion has extended itself in some measure throughout our whole being. If sin were the color blue, I would be some shade of blue all over. Even in my best deeds there is a discoloration of self-centeredness instead of God-centeredness.[12]

Even in my most humble attempt to serve others selflessly, there is likely some trace of selfishness mixed in my motive. The only way to reduce selfishness is to remember that true service is clearly focused on the whos, and ultimately on Who: *He must become greater; I must become less* (John 3:30).

One of the surest indications of blurry focus brought on by selfishness is anger toward others, which leads to unforgiveness, bitterness, and division. Have you ever heard the phrase, "I was so angry that I saw red." Consider this: "Some people literally see red [when triggered by extreme anger] because the rush of blood being pumped far too quickly and powerfully expands the capillaries in their eyes."[13] Now that is blurry vision!

When I competed in karate, I had an advantage when my opponent became angry because his anger stole vital focusing resources from him. Anger is a serious issue for some Christians and for some Christian school educators, although the Bible is clear on this subject.

> *My dear brothers and sisters, take note of this: Everyone should be quick to listen, slow to speak and slow to become angry, because human anger does not produce the righteousness that God desires.* (James 1:19-20)

The last part of this verse is so instructive. We actually stop the production of righteousness in our relationships when we become angry. James elaborated by asking this insightful question: *What causes fights and quarrels among you? Don't they come from your desires that battle within you? You want something but don't get it* (James 4:1-2). This is pure selfishness.

I sometimes illustrate the damaging effect of anger by simply turning off the light switch in a roomful of people. Then I ask, "Is the electricity still available to power the light bulbs over our heads?" Yes. But I have interrupted the flow of electricity to the light bulbs by means of a toggle switch. The power to light the room is still available, but I chose to impede its ability. Anger is like that electrical switch in our relationships—it interrupts the flow of spiritual connectivity with others until we choose to turn it back on, reengaging the source of power.

Some people may argue that anger is a justifiable reaction to the offenses of others. They emphasize that Jesus Himself became angry when He cleansed the temple (Matt. 21:12-13). They may refer to this as righteous indignation. While the word *anger* or *wrath* is not specifically mentioned in this scriptural account, Jesus displayed a holy zeal when He drove out those who were turning His Father's house into a den of thieves. He had reason to do so. The moneychangers had become an obstacle to those who were trying to bring their sacrificial offerings to God to be forgiven of their sins (Matt. 21:12; Mark 11:15; Luke 19:45; John 2:13). Jesus wanted to clear the way for people to enter the presence of God.

When I am honest, I admit that there have been few times (if any) in my entire life that my anger has been holy or righteous. When I see red, my anger is sinful and ungodly. Moreover, it has cut off the righteousness production in my relationship with a significant person (a who) in my life and ministry. *People with understanding control their anger; a hot temper shows great foolishness* (Prov. 14:29 NLT). Left unresolved, anger leads to unforgiveness, bitterness, and division.

What threatens the effectiveness of Christian school ministry more than anything else? The answer is unforgiveness, which results in bitterness and division. How tragic is it that we, who have received so much mercy and forgiveness, continue to harbor unforgiveness toward others *for whom Christ died* (1 Cor. 8:11)?

This type of blurry focus from the selfishness of denying forgiveness to others actually causes ministry blindness—a condition that disallows true Christian service. Think about it—the message of the gospel is forgiveness. *Be kind and compassionate to one another, forgiving each other, just as in Christ God forgave you* (Eph. 4:32). Jesus taught us to pray, "*Forgive us our debts as we also have forgiven our debtors*" (Matt. 6:12). Perhaps one of the most important things we can do to improve our focus in Christian school ministry is to forgive someone. Francis Schaeffer said, "Many Christians rarely or never seem to connect their own lack of reality of fellowship with God with their lack of forgiveness to men."[14]

Unforgiveness produces bitterness. No one likes bitterness. It is most reprehensible when it is displayed by someone in Christian ministry. Yet we have all encountered bitter people. They either have a sour disposition that comes across as hostile toward others, or they manifest a self-righteous, silent-treatment bitterness that is arrogant and dismissive. Webster defines bitterness as "exhibiting intense animosity accompanied by severe pain and suffering." The Bible says that bitterness is a poisonous root that grows to cause trouble and defile others (Heb. 12:15). Bitterness is a synonym for resentment.

> Resentment is when you let your hurt become hate. Resentment is when you poke, stoke, feed, and fan the fire, stirring the flames and reliving the pain…. Resentment is the deliberate decision to nurse the offense until it becomes a black, furry, growling grudge.[15]

I would not wish bitterness on my worst enemy if I had one. But bitterness is more common in our Christian schools than we like to admit. It results in division, our enemy's most effective weapon against us. If he can keep us fighting with each other, our focus will always be blurry, and we will not have any time left to focus on the whos. Ephesians 4:1-3 is our focusing knob for selfishness:

> *I urge you to live a life worthy of the calling you have received. Be completely humble and gentle; be patient, bearing with one another in love. Make every effort to keep the unity of the Spirit through the bond of peace.*

The cure for selfishness begins with humility:

> Humility is a perfect quietness of heart. It is to expect nothing, to wonder at nothing that is done to me, to feel nothing done against me. It is to be at rest when nobody praises me, and when I am blamed or despised. It is to have a blessed home in the Lord, where I can go in and shut the door, and kneel to my Father in secret, and am at peace as in a deep sea of calmness, when all around and above is trouble.[16]

# Weariness Causes Blurry Focus

*We must not become tired of doing good. We will
receive our harvest of eternal life at the right time
if we do not give up.* Galatians 6:9 (NCV)

One of the greatest honors of my life was serving in the United States Marine Corps when President Ronald Reagan was the Commander in Chief of our armed forces. During my two enlistments in the 1980s, although we were not actively engaged in any full-scale wars, I was deployed four different times on US Navy ships to various regions of the western Pacific and Indian Oceans as well as to the Mediterranean Sea. President Reagan used Marines as a show of force in highly visible combined-forces training exercises near hot spots around the world. I was a squad leader in an infantry helicopter assault unit, so these exercises, such as Cobra Gold (a multi-nation military exercise still held annually), were quite exciting. They included impressive close air support, powerful naval gunfire, imposing mechanized armor, along with a variety of other supporting assets. I will never forget my experience during one of these training missions in a remote jungle region of Thailand near the borders of Cambodia and Vietnam.

On an extremely hot, humid day, we made the one-hour journey from sea to land via a CH-46 helicopter (a troop-carrier with two overhead rotors). We were coming from the *USS Belleau Wood*, a Landing Helicopter Assault (LHA) ship we affectionately called a baby aircraft carrier. As part of a Marine Expeditionary Unit, our company's mission was to secure a particular ridgeline on a mountain range overlooking miles of rice paddies in the valley below. From this position, we were to conduct patrols to prevent the enemy aggressors from gaining access to the main objective via the mountain passes. This was a familiar mission for Kilo Company, 3rd Battalion, 3rd Marines—one we had performed many times in many places.

As the squad leader, I had to determine where to land the "bird"—close enough to reach our position in the mountains, but also remote enough to ensure my men could disembark safely. I was a trained land navigator, but from the air, all the mountain ranges and rice paddy valleys looked quite similar. I consulted with the pilot and, against his advice, chose to land in a small field with high grass in a lower region of the training sector to conceal our presence. I thought it would be better to be a little further from our objective if we could land undetected. The landing was unopposed, and we were soon making our way through a valley of deep jungle undergrowth. I had underestimated how difficult it would be to cut a path through the high brush toward the mountain range that looked much further away once we were on the ground. I learned later that we had actually landed seventeen "clicks" (thousand yard increments) farther south than scheduled. I wish I had heeded the pilot's advice.

The heat was unbearable with temperatures above 100 degrees Fahrenheit along with high humidity that hung heavy in the air. Loaded down with heavy packs and weapons, we were all soaking wet with perspiration within a few minutes. Although we carried extra water, I knew our supply would not last long at the rate we were going. And the mosquitoes. I do not have adequate words to describe what it feels like to be eaten alive—but I digress.

After eight grueling hours of trudging through high grass, swampy bottoms, and triple canopy jungle, we crossed a maze of rice paddy dikes to reach the bottom of the mountain range. By this point, I could see the effects of heat exhaustion impacting my men. My head was pounding from the heat; I felt weak, nauseous, and physically overwhelmed. By my calculations, we had arrived at our first checkpoint—the one we were supposed to make soon after landing that morning. We still had ten clicks to go, and they were all uphill. My platoon commander was livid that we had not arrived at our assigned position. Through the radio, he made it clear that he did not appreciate our "lollygagging around all day to see the sights of Thailand" while the rest of our platoon was digging in for the night. How could I tell him that it would be after midnight before we arrived?

What happened next is embedded in my memory, as if it happened yesterday (although it was over thirty years ago). "The men are spent—they need a break," one of my team leaders reported to me. He was a fine Marine, not one to ever complain, and I knew he was right.

"We have to climb this mountain first," I replied, trying to hide my exhaustion. With little persuasion, he convinced me to give the men a few minutes of well-deserved rest before the arduous climb. I felt guilty that I had put them in this position, so I agreed to a ten-minute break. Before I could blink, my normally well-disciplined Marines had picked out a shady spot beside a stream, and they were jettisoning their packs, pulling off their helmets, and laying down their rifles (an absolute never for combat-trained Marines). Several took off their boots to put their feet in the cool water. I knew better, but I did not have the heart to stop them. Everything in my training told me that we needed to spread out, take up defensive positions, and stay alert. We also needed to send out a small reconnaissance patrol to ensure we were in a secure place. But I was weary and my focus was blurry.

It happened almost in slow motion. A canister flew through the air, a stream of red smoke pouring out behind it. It landed with a thump in the middle of my squad. Smoke billowed and enveloped the men. Simultaneously, the loud and rhythmic sound of a machine gun opened up a few yards away as enemy aggressors poured out of the surrounding jungle forest, firing their rifles (with blank ammunition since it was a training exercise) at close range into my unprepared and unprotected men.

"We're hit. We're hit!" my radioman yelled into the handset before I could give him any instructions. "We're all down—all wiped out," he said despondently in answer to the platoon commander's inquiry of our status. Everything was over in less than a minute—my entire squad eliminated. While it was only a training exercise, I can still feel the intense sting of that moment as I share it with you.

I made many mistakes that day—mistakes in training that my platoon commander ensured would serve to steel my resolve as a leader to never put my Marines in a position like that again, no matter how weary they became under the strain of circumstance. That valuable lesson would save lives in real, future situations.

Weariness is real, and it has a real effect on us. Life can be difficult on any given day, and those of us who have been called to serve in Christian school ministry will likely become weary. Weariness results from a variety of circumstances—the busyness of our workload, strained resources, difficult people, as well as personal and family struggles. Weariness causes our focus to become blurry, and, as a result, we often make poor decisions that negatively affect others. When we are weary, we tend to become preoccupied with the tough circumstances, difficult people, and complicated challenges of Christian ministry. When these things consume our mind and our energy, little room is left to focus on the true purpose of our calling.

What happened to me on that fateful day in Thailand can also happen to us in our Christian schools. We can create issues or make decisions that leave us mired in difficult situations. We then expend much of our energy (and the energy of others) wading through the circumstances we have created for ourselves by moving outside our areas of accountability. Sometimes we are assigned to follow others in authority who make this kind of poor decision, and we are relegated to endure the misery they have created for us. Then we become exhausted; we lose our focus and let down our guard, allowing the enemy to ambush us along with those entrusted to our care.

Christian school educators often tell me about their weariness and their heavy burdens. When I stop and pray with them in the midst of these conversations, this verse often comes to mind:

> *Jesus said, "Come to me, all of you who are weary and carry heavy burdens, and I will give you rest. Take my yoke upon you. Let me teach you, because I am humble and gentle at heart, and you will find rest for your souls. For my yoke is easy to bear, and the burden I give you is light.* (Matt. 11:28-30 NLT)

Jesus offers rest for our souls, an easy yoke, and a light burden. So why are God's people, who are called to serve Him in the ministry of Christian education, so tired and heavy laden? Maybe we are exhausted because many of the burdens we carry are self-imposed or self-inflicted. Jesus has not assigned us a heavy burden, so if we are feeling weary in Christian ministry, it is likely because we have taken on more than He has asked us to carry.

I often remind myself that I can be responsible only for that which I have been granted responsibility. That may sound simplistic, but far too often we become obsessed with circumstances and people God has not assigned to us. He has actually called others, sometimes those in authority over us, to carry that burden. But for some reason, we assume responsibility for something we were not given to carry. Sadly, when we become weary from trying to carry burdens God has not assigned to us, we often become too weary to carry the ones He has assigned. If you are weary today, please hear Jesus saying, "*My burden is light,*" and unload the cart of things He has not asked you to carry (Matt. 11:30).

My grandfather was a woodworker. He made a small replica of an oxen yoke to remind me that I am yoked with Jesus. He told me that when a young ox is being trained, it is yoked together with an older, more experienced ox. The older one pulls the weight while the younger one simply walks along beside him, learning effortlessly. Being yoked with Jesus means that we are not supposed to be pulling ahead of Him or lagging behind Him. We are to walk alongside Him at His pace. When done correctly, this is easy. If you are not finding ministry easy, allow the Holy Spirit to help you *keep in step* in your walk alongside Jesus (Gal. 5:25). And do not forget to fix your eyes on Jesus in the process so you *will not grow weary and lose heart* (Heb. 12:3). That is the best cure for blurry focus caused by weariness.

## Worry Causes Blurry Focus

*Peace I leave with you; my peace I give you. I do not
give to you as the world gives. Do not let your hearts
be troubled and do not be afraid.* John 14:27

The English word *worry* comes from the German word for *strangle* or *choke*.
Worry can choke the joy out of our lives.

> Worry is fear's extravagance. It extracts interest on trouble
> before it comes due. It constantly drains the energy God
> gives us to face daily problems and to fulfill our many
> responsibilities. It is therefore a sinful waste.[17]

Worry may come from an excessive focus on the whats instead of the whos.
Don't worry—be happy. It sounds so simple. But when we realize that the
biblical word for worrying refers to fretting fearfully about a matter—or
anxiousness—that sounds more serious. Anxious thoughts are the mental
gymnastics we host in our minds about various issues. These thoughts
hinder our ability to focus by constantly diverting our attention as we roll
things over and over in our minds. *Worry weighs a person down* (Prov. 12:25
NLT). Perry Noble says,

> We get so focused on our circumstances that we can't
> focus on Christ. Focusing on our circumstances and the
> size of our problems always leads to stress, anxiety, and
> fear…. The enemy doesn't want us to focus on Christ or
> His word. He wants us to focus on our circumstances. If
> He can get us to focus on our circumstances, He can keep
> us in bondage to worry, fear, and anxiety.[18]

We know worry is actually fear—we do not trust in the Lord with all our
heart, and instead, we rely on our own understanding (Prov. 3:5-6). We
also know that anxious thoughts occur because we are not prayerfully
allowing God's peace to guard our hearts and minds (Phil. 4: 6-7). Richard
Blackaby explains where the problem lies:

> We serve a God so powerful He created an entire universe out of nothing. He holds every star and galaxy in its place. He took a lump of clay and created a living human being. He gives life to every person on earth… there is nothing God cannot do. Yet sadly, despite the fathomless potential for Christians to experience God's power, many continue to live in defeat and discouragement. The problem is never with God. God has proven throughout history that no human condition or situation exceeds His ability to do a miracle. The limiting factor is always us.[19]

So how do we stop worrying? Paul instructs us to *capture every thought and make it give up and obey Christ* (2 Cor. 10:5 NCV). Paul uses the Greek word *aichmalotos* for the word *captive*. It literally means to lead a captured prisoner away at the point of a spear.[20] That is a thought-provoking word picture. Instead of allowing our worries or anxious thoughts to capture us, we should capture them. I give myself a simple challenge when anxious thoughts are persistent: Attempt to pray about the matter more than thinking (or talking) about it. I am not very good at doing this, but attempting it improves my prayer life. It helps to remember to cast all my anxieties on Jesus, because He cares for me (1 Peter 5:7). It also helps to remember that when things are difficult for me, they are never too difficult for God (Jer. 32:17). Sometimes, a simple but powerful prayer is all that is needed to bring about a clear focus: Lord, *we do not know what to do, but our eyes are upon you* (2 Chron. 20:12).

Psalm 139 has been a great help when I am captivated by worry or anxious thoughts. In this psalm, David acknowledged how the Lord searched him and knew him and how the Lord was familiar with everything in his life. He recognized that the Lord completely hemmed him in behind and before. David could not escape from His Spirit because His right hand held him fast. David concluded, *Such knowledge is too wonderful for me; it is high; I cannot attain it* (Ps. 139:6 ESV). Knowing that God is intimately acquainted with me and with every circumstance in my life brings comfort and peace beyond comprehension. David closed Psalm 139 with a prayer:

*Search me, God, and know my heart; test me and know my anxious thoughts. See if there is any offensive way in me, and lead me in the way everlasting.* (ESV)

We must allow the Holy Spirit to search our hearts and expose any worries or anxious thoughts. We need to allow Him to look for any offensive ways (perhaps the sin of trusting ourselves more than trusting Him) and let Him lead us in His way.

*Finally, brothers and sisters, whatever is true, whatever is noble, whatever is right, whatever is pure, whatever is lovely, whatever is admirable—if anything is excellent or praiseworthy—think about such things. Whatever you have learned or received or heard from me, or seen in me—put it into practice. And the God of peace will be with you.* (Phil. 4:8-9)

# Distractions Cause Blurry Focus

*Keep your eyes straight ahead; ignore all sideshow distractions.* Proverbs 4:25 (MSG)

Clear focus is not easy to maintain even in perfect conditions. How much more difficult is it to focus when we are surrounded constantly by a multitude of distractions? Even if we could somehow eliminate the detrimental distractions, plenty of harmless distractions could still break our focus. As I type this paragraph, it is almost impossible to ignore the e-mail icon on my computer screen, which tells me that new e-mails await my attention. These e-mails could contain something important or something completely insignificant (electronic junk mail), but the icon does not distinguish this for me. It just dutifully informs me that my attention is needed elsewhere. And that icon is only one distraction among many.

Distractions divide our focus among a number of things at once so we end up focusing on those things instead of on our primary purpose. Phillip May says,

> Today's educators are like the field general who has become
> so involved in the problems and tactics of the immediate
> battle that he neglects the overall strategy of the war, and
> may even have forgotten why it is being fought.[21]

Some distractions come from the enemy: storms, attacks, division, confusion, deception, or fear. But other distractions come from our lack of spiritual discipline. We can become intoxicated with selfish pleasure, pride, ambition, money, or a quest for power. We also can become distracted by the busyness of Christian ministry to the point that we focus more on our to-do lists than on the whos that the to-dos were intended to serve. Whatever the case, distractions are a constant, and they blur our focus.

On that incredible day crossing the Sea of Galilee, the disciples had many distractions—travel weariness from rowing, bailing water out of the boat during the storm, the demon-possessed man, the bleeding woman, and Jarius. Therefore, they lost their focus on Jesus and the whos that needed help. As Christian school educators, we also lose sight of Jesus and His focus in the day-to-day realities of our ministry. We often focus on our own lack of comfort or convenience instead of the one who needs to be rescued. We become preoccupied with the menial aspects of our work: lesson planning, grading responsibilities, parent conferences, fundraisers, discipline issues, and extra-curricular activities. Like the disciples, sometimes we simply want the day to end so we can go home and rest. Sadly, we give our time and attention to things related to what may be easier, more comfortable, or more interesting rather than devote our time and energy to people who may not seem grateful for our efforts.

How do we remedy the blurry focus that results from distractions? It is vital that we find a way to focus on the whos in the midst of all the competing whats. We must train ourselves to hear God's voice above all the noise of our circumstances.

A story is told, perhaps apocryphal since the source is unknown, about a young man who applied for a job as a Morse code operater for a telegraph company. When he arrived for the interview, he was asked to wait in a large, noisy area with the other applicants. In the background, he heard a telegraph clacking away. A sign on the receptionist's counter instructed job applicants to fill out a form and wait until they were summoned to enter the inner office.

Suddenly, the young man stood up and walked right into the inner office. The other applicants were surprised that he had been so bold, and they assumed his presumptiousness would disqualify him for the job. Instead, he emerged from the inner office moments later escorted by the employer, who announced excitedly the job had been filled. The other applicants began to complain because they had not been interviewed for the job. The employer responded, "All the time you've been sitting here, the telegraph has been ticking out the following message in Morse code: 'If you understand this message, then come right in. The job is yours.' None of you heard it or understood it. This young man did. So the job is his."

The young man in this story was able to eliminate all the distractions so he could decode the instructions that were being given. He was able to do it because he recognized the voice and focused on the message. Jesus said, *"My sheep recognize my voice. I know them, and they follow me"* (John 10:27 MSG). To be effective in our ministry in Christian education, it is imperative that we focus our attention on Who. In all the noise that surrounds us, are we able to see His face and hear His voice? Only then we will be able to filter out the distractions and focus on the whos He has called us to serve.

# CHAPTER 7

# Clear Focus

*Concentrate all of your thoughts on the work at hand.*
*The sun's rays do not burn until brought to a focus.*
Alexander Graham Bell[22]

Cold rain was falling, and a small gust of wind occasionally blew raindrops onto the side of my face. A slight chill rippled through my body as I lay on the wet ground in the prone position on a firing range at Marine Corps Base Camp Lejeune in North Carolina. *This is my day,* I thought as I made one final adjustment to the sights of my M14 rifle. Twenty accurate shots from 600 yards, and my team would win the match.

I was fortunate enough to have been selected for the Camp Lejeune Rifle and Pistol Team, although I was not as skilled as many of my teammates. The competition we faced was fierce, not only with the other armed forces teams, but also with the civilian shooters who participated in the matches. Many of our competitors had more expensive weapons with high-tech sighting equipment along with all the other bells and whistles. Our team used only stock, match-grade rifles with open sights (no scopes) because everyone knows that United States Marines are the best shots in the world. Ooh-rah!

Miserable-weather days were my best opportunity to compete with some of the finest competitive marksmen in our region. And rain with wind gave me the advantage I needed. The prima donna shooters would be distracted by this kind of weather; keeping their expensive equipment dry and their scopes from fogging would preoccupy them. The other armed forces teams would likely want to shoot their yard lines faster so they could get out of the elements and back to the comfort of their bases. But our Marine Corps team lived for weather like this—after all, we were trained to be amphibious. Our drill instructors at Parris Island had ensured that we not only could endure inclement weather but also would learn to prefer it.

*Focus*, I kept telling myself.

Everything around me screamed the opposite. The cold, wet ground seemed to draw out my body heat like a vacuum. The cloudy conditions restricted much-needed light in my rifle sights and reduced target visibility. The splashing of raindrops on my rifle barrel created a miniature water show, which competed for my auditory and visual attention. The frigid wind pushed against my body and rifle with inconsistent gusts. I braced myself against what felt like an invisible competitor.

*Focus*, I repeated, attempting to calmly silence the multitude of distractions.

Then my training took over, my mind forcing my body to perform something I had practiced hundreds of times. Mentally, I rehearsed the words my marksmanship instructor had repeated over and over: *Focus on the clear tip of the front sight post, centered in the rear sight aperture.*

My mind flashed back to my introduction to the M14 rifle. Near the end of the rifle barrel, the now-familiar front sight post was the characteristic of the weapon my instructors had emphasized most. On the other end of the rifle, in front of the stock, the rear sight aperture was much more interesting to examine. It looked like a tiny open scope (without glass or cross hairs) for the shooter to look through to align the rifle with the target. For an accurate shot, the shooter had to look through the rear sight aperture while centering the clear tip of the front sight post on the blurry target down range. Simple, yes, but difficult to do in these conditions.

From 600 yards away, the twelve-inch bull's-eye on the target looked like the head of a pin. But focus is the key. Relax, breathe, and apply steady trigger pressure until—

BOOM!

The rifle exploded with such force it surprised me. Perfect. That is exactly what is supposed to happen. I was quickly rewarded with a target marked with a white spotter in the middle of the bull's-eye. Only nineteen more to go.

That day, I recorded my best competitive score from the 600-yard line—twenty bull's-eyes, twelve in the six-inch center x-ring—enough to help our team win the overall match.

A clear focus can be rewarding in any setting, but more so when something eternal is at stake. As Christian school educators, our target is not made of paper, and our score is not calculated with numbers. We affect the lives of our students with every opportunity God gives us to influence them for the sake of Jesus Christ. We must not fail to maintain a clear focus so we can see them through Jesus' eyes of faith, love them with His compassion, and serve them in His strength.

# Clear Focus Requires Faith

> *So if you're serious about living this new resurrection life*
> *with Christ, act like it. Pursue the things over which Christ*
> *presides. Don't shuffle along, eyes to the ground, absorbed*
> *with the things right in front of you. Look up, and be alert to*
> *what is going on around Christ—that's where the action is.*
> *See things from his perspective.* Colossians 3:1-2 (MSG)

Focus must have an object. We cannot focus clearly on a wide spectrum of things. Sure, we can see a wide spectrum; and with keen observation, we can take in much information through our eyes. But to truly focus on something clearly, we have to use more than our eyes. Our minds have to discard other thoughts and focus on the one thing. We have to tune all our senses toward the object and away from distracting things that are part of the overall picture.

As previously established, this can be quite difficult because many things compete for our attention. However, we can focus on a person much easier than other things because God designed us to focus our attention on Him and on other people made in His image and likeness. This presents a difficulty for us. We cannot physically see Jesus, but we do have the eyewitness accounts of those in the Bible who did. We can use their descriptions to paint a mental image. For example, John writes about the disciples using their physical senses to see and experience Jesus:

> *That which was from the beginning, which we have heard,*
> *which we have seen with our eyes, which we have looked at*
> *and our hands have touched—this we proclaim concerning*
> *the Word of life. The life appeared; we have seen it and testify*
> *to it, and we proclaim to you the eternal life, which was with*
> *the Father and has appeared to us.* (1 John 1:1-2)

Unlike the disciples, we cannot use our five physical senses to focus our attention on Jesus. We are able, however, to use our physical senses to focus on other people. Unfortunately, we often see them in their sinful condition (or in some degree of imperfection), so it may be difficult to focus on their potential and to remember they have been created in the image and likeness of God. So how do we properly focus on Who (and who)? How can we focus on something we cannot see?

This is precisely what we are called to do—to see the unseen through eyes of faith. Paul wrote, *So we fix our eyes not on what is seen, but on what is unseen, since what is seen is temporary, but what is unseen is eternal* (2 Cor. 4:18). Fixing our eyes on what is unseen is the key to maintaining a clear focus in Christian ministry—and doing so requires faith. *Faith means being sure of the things we hope for and knowing that something is real even if we do not see it* (Heb. 11:1 NCV). We can focus on God by faith, and we can focus on others by faith, looking with expectancy to see what God can do in and through their lives.

First, we need to fix our eyes on Jesus, the *champion who initiates and perfects our faith* (Heb. 12:2 NLT). Our clear focus originates in Jesus and He sustains it. But how can we fix our eyes on Jesus when we cannot physically see Him? By faith. Thomas initially doubted Jesus' resurrection, so Jesus told him, *"Because you have seen me, you have believed; blessed are those who have not seen and yet have believed"* (John 20:29). Jesus was blessing us—those who believe in Him although we have not physically seen Him.

Peter echoed this truth when he wrote, *though you have not seen Him, you love Him, and though you do not see Him now, but believe in Him, you greatly rejoice with joy inexpressible and full of glory, obtaining as the outcome of your faith the salvation of your souls* (1 Peter 1:8-9 NASB). I love the clear message of this verse—love produced by faith results in inexpressible joy in our salvation. This was the experience of the Old Testament heroes of the faith catalogued in Hebrews 11. Noah, Abraham, Moses, and many others are heralded for their ability to see through eyes of faith what they could not physically see. Jesus said, *"Abraham rejoiced as he looked forward to my coming. He saw it and was glad"* (John 8:56 NLT).

What is the source of this kind of faith?

These exemplary models of faith were able to focus on invisible, eternal things in the midst of seemingly impossible visible circumstances. They developed an ability to focus on the evidence (or court-worthy proof) by closing their physical eyes of understanding and opening their spiritual eyes and ears to receive the message God had spoken to them.

We too can learn to see the unseen by focusing on the evidence of God's spoken word. Think of it—everything we see with our visible eyes originated from that which was invisible. How? By God's spoken word: *God said, "Let there be light," and there was light* (Gen. 1:3). He *spoke* things into visibility. Since we have a record of what God has said—the Word of God—we can see Him. He has revealed Himself to us through what He spoke into existence (Rom. 1:20).

The men and women of faith listed in Hebrews 11 saw eternal things by fixing their eyes of faith on what God had told them. Amazingly, they did not receive the promises they were given (Heb. 11:39). We do, though—in the Word of God Himself, our Lord Jesus Christ. *The Word became flesh and made his dwelling among us. We have seen his glory, the glory of the one and only Son, who came from the Father, full of grace and truth* (John 1:14). Jesus is the Word. He is the evidence. This is why He is the author and finisher of our faith, worthy of our full and complete focus.

In the marksmanship illustration at the beginning of this chapter, I mentioned that we were trained to focus on the clear tip of the front sight post of the rifle. When we did that, the target remained blurry in the sight picture behind it. This would seem illogical to someone who has never fired a rifle. A novice shooter typically focuses on the target; however, the human eye can focus clearly on only one object at a time. If the shooter's focus is directed toward the target, the rifle sights will drift, causing inaccurate shots. So the shooter's primary focus must be fixed on the clear tip of the front sight post while he maintains sight alignment with the target.

In the same way, to be effective in hitting our target as Christian school educators, we have to train ourselves to develop a clear focus on Jesus first, with our students in the sight picture behind Him. He is our focal point. As we do this, we will see that His attention—His focus—is on our students, thus making it possible for us to impact their lives for eternity. Also, as we model this kind of focus, our students will learn to imitate us, enabling them to keep Jesus in their focus as well.

Simeon and Anna are wonderful examples of this kind of clear focus. The story of these two extraordinary people is told in Luke 2:22-38. Simeon was a righteous and devout man, and the Holy Spirit was upon him as he waited for God to fulfill His promise to see the consolation of

Israel. Anna was a prophetess who worshiped day and night, fasting and praying in the temple. Both of them were dedicated, attentive worshipers. It would have been easy to miss the Messiah in a busy place like the temple with so many religious activities going on—circumcisions, purifications, sacrifices, and much more. It also would have been easy for Simeon and Anna to focus on outward appearance as they searched the crowds daily for the promised Savior. But they did not miss Jesus; they recognized Him, they praised and thanked God, and announced Jesus to others in the temple. They focused their attention and the attention of others on Jesus.

Some historians believe that Rembrandt, the famous Dutch painter, may have spent the final years of his life fixated on this scene at the temple with Simeon and Anna. He painted several canvases of the scene, and his last unfinished painting, found in his studio after his death, was of Simeon holding the baby Jesus in his arms. Perhaps as Rembrandt grew older, he began to realize the significance of fixing his own eyes on Jesus, the author and finisher of his faith.[23]

John the Baptist is another example of this kind of clear focus. In the midst of his busy ministry—preaching about the Kingdom of God and baptizing people—he focused his attention and the attention of his disciples on Jesus:

> *The next day John saw Jesus coming toward him and said, "Look, the Lamb of God, who takes away the sin of the world!"* (John 1:29)

> *The next day John was there again with two of his disciples. When he saw Jesus passing by, he said, "Look, the Lamb of God!" When the two disciples heard him say this, they followed Jesus.* (John 1:35-37)

John the Baptist was clearly focused on Jesus. He was looking for Him, and when he saw Him, his first response was to tell others to look on Jesus as well. Tim LaHaye, in his book, *Jesus*, says:

> Sadly, the religious leaders of the day completely missed the boat. The very group who more than any other should

have recognized the appearance of the Messiah because of their "knowledge" of the Scriptures refused to accept Him. In fact, when Jesus arrived on the scene years later as an adult, they were quite hostile to say the least. And it wasn't simply a lack of knowledge or unfamiliarity with Scriptures that was the problem. For them, it was a matter of the heart, not the head.[24]

Jesus is the focal point of all history. We cannot afford to miss Him. Looking for Him, recognizing Him, and clearly keeping Him in view purifies our focus and makes us effective in Christian ministry. Can you hear Him saying, *"If you look for me wholeheartedly, you will find me. I will be found by you"?* (Jer. 29:13 NLT).

# Clear Focus Is Always about Producing Life

*I came to give life—life in all its fullness.* John 10:10 (NCV)

Once we clearly see through eyes of faith because we understand the source is found in God's Word—in Jesus—we can begin to focus on the whos in our lives that God wants to rescue and restore. God's agenda is always about producing life. This is illustrated perfectly in that incredible day with Jesus and His disciples on the Sea of Galilee. Jesus saved the lives of each person in the four encounters Mark described: He saved the disciples' lives by rescuing them from the storm. He saved the demon-possessed man's life by casting out the demons. He saved the life of the woman with the issue of blood. And He saved the life of Jairus's daughter—by bringing her back to life.

The fact that God's agenda is to produce life should not surprise us. From the creation of the world, through the incarnation and resurrection of Jesus, and forever in eternity, God is producing life. He is the giver and sustainer of all life. He desires to give eternal life to all those who believe in the gift of His Son (John 3:16). This is a helpful clue for us as we serve God in Christian ministry. Whenever we focus on a who, we can be sure that God is working to either provide or restore life. Jesus said that He came to give us abundant life (John 10:10).

Peter grew to understand this fact. When we find him in Lydda (near Joppa) in Acts 9, we see how far he had come since he first met Jesus. Luke's record of what happened in Joppa is stunning. But to fully appreciate it, we should review Luke's description of Peter's progression in his ability to focus on whos.

Luke seemed to enjoy providing details about Peter. Perhaps it was Peter's colorful personality or his willingness to express what everyone else was thinking. It also may have been Peter's willingness to act boldly on what he believed, giving Luke the power of story in his writing. At any rate, Luke provides some amazing details about Peter's life and ministry in his gospel as well as in the Acts of the Apostles.

Luke's introduction of Simon Peter is fascinating. A common fisherman is washing his nets on the shore of the Sea of Galilee after a wasted night of fishing—not a single fish to show for it. Jesus walked up, climbed into

Simon Peter's boat and asked him to push off a little from the shore so He could teach the crowds. Can you envision it?

I have stood on docks and watched fishermen return from fishing expeditions. A dock does not seem like the kind of place one would expect to hear a sermon. And unless you are a customer, fishermen are not typically hospitable—especially if you want to use their boat for your own purposes. But Peter must have recognized Jesus' authority because he immediately complied; he put out into the deep water and let down his nets again. *"Because you say so, I will let down the nets,"* he said (Luke 5:5). When the nets nearly broke from the large catch, Peter fell at Jesus' knees and said, *"Go away from me, Lord; I am a sinful man!"* (Luke 5:8).

But Jesus said to him, *"Don't be afraid; from now on you will fish for people"* (Luke 5:10). Peter believed, and then he immediately left everything to become Jesus' disciple. At that point, his new life began.

Not long after this experience, Peter was sailing to the other side of the Sea of Galilee with his fellow disciples and Jesus. At the end of that incredible day, he was privileged to enter Jairus's house and witness Jesus raising his daughter from the dead (Luke 8:51-56). Peter saw many of Jesus' miracles, including a widow's son being raised from the dead in a town called Nain (Luke 7:14-15), Lazarus being raised from the dead (John 11:43), and, of course, the resurrection of Jesus Himself. Peter was the first disciple to arrive at the empty tomb (Luke 24:12). He fully understood that Jesus was the Messiah who had come to give life—he had watched it happen.

So years later, when the disciples sent for Peter in Lydda, near Joppa, he arrived at a familiar scene (Acts 9:36-42). Tabitha, a well-known and much beloved follower of Jesus, had become sick and died. Evidently, she had made a huge impact on her community—especially with her ability to sew and make clothes for the poor. The grief over her premature death overwhelmed those who knew and loved her. Peter knew exactly what to do because he had been with Jesus on several occasions in almost identical circumstances. He cleared the room, got down on his knees and prayed, then turned to Tabitha and told her to get up. She did. Peter's clear focus was producing life.

One way to ensure that our focus always produces life is to ask these questions: What does abundant life look like for the who in front of me? Is it the need for salvation—eternal life? Is it the need for freedom from the bondage of sin—victorious life? Is it the need for peace and relief related to a health concern, a financial burden, or a broken relationship—abundant life?

Then with eyes of faith see how Jesus can bring abundant life.

He may use you to do it.

# Clear Focus Has Compassion for the Desperate

*Because of the LORD's great love we are not consumed, for*
*his compassions never fail. They are new every morning;*
*great is your faithfulness.* Lamentations 3:22-23

Compassion is defined as "a feeling of deep sympathy or sorrow for another who is stricken with misfortune, accompanied by the strong desire to alleviate the suffering."[25] It is "a form of love, aroused within us when we are confronted with those who suffer or are vulnerable."[26]

Another way to evaluate the clarity of our focus in ministry is to examine our compassion for the desperate whos in our life. Compassion was a signature characteristic of Jesus' ministry when He lived on earth. He was always attentive to those who were oppressed, hurting, and broken. He was never too tired or too busy to stop what He was doing to meet the needs of desperate people. Sometimes our ministry duties (often, an obsessive focus on whats instead of whos) seem so significant that we do not listen to desperate people with a compassionate heart. But compassion can be a barometer of our focus: if we do not have compassion, our focus has likely changed from whos to whats. Consider a hypothetical example:

> Ricky is the star quarterback on your school's football team. With his skill, he is certain to help you win the championship this year. Several universities are already recruiting him as a potential scholarship prospect. Life is good for you as the head football coach. But everything changes in an instant with one blindside tackle. With a broken collarbone, Ricky is unable to play for the rest of the season. As the head football coach, where is your focus? Hopefully, it is on the who. The compassion barometer is an ongoing measurement of this focus. At first, as Ricky experiences serious pain, compassion is a natural response. Perhaps when you see him standing on the sidelines during the next game, you think, *Poor Ricky. I know he wishes he could participate in this game, especially since a recruiter was scheduled to watch him play.*

But other football games are scheduled, and many other coaching responsibilities require your attention. You must also coach a new quarterback. What is your compassion barometer reading one week later? One month later? Is it still showing who or has it changed to what?

This type of scenario can play out in many different ways in our Christian schools on any given day. Teachers, support staff, coaches, or leaders constantly face various situations that require them to focus on a desperate who. Yet the ministry requirements do not pause during this time. The homework still needs to be graded. The lesson plans, quizzes, and tests still need to be prepared. Deadlines are not delayed. Programs, budgets, meetings, people, and problems continue to demand our attention. Our focus is continuously challenged. But what is the compassion barometer reading for those around us who may be in crisis? In these times of desperation, deep spiritual transformation often occurs.

Todd Marrah has done extensive research with thousands of students in Christian schools in the area of spiritual formation. He found that crisis often plays a critical role in their spiritual growth:

> There is a tremendous opportunity for crisis-related spiritual growth if our schools can continue to find ways to help students deepen their relationship with God through their suffering.... Suffering is one of the most transformative opportunities in the Christian life because it often gives us access to deep places in our soul that we would not otherwise know existed. Trials shake up our negative gut-level expectations of God and other important people in our lives. Working through trials, however, always occurs in the context of relationships and community. Relationships change our brain, our soul, and our ability to love.[27]

When people are in difficult or desperate situations, their spiritual growth potential is high. Jesus knew this; therefore, His compassion for desperate people was endless. He gave Himself completely to nourish, rescue, and protect those who had no other hope. Jesus extended His compassion to vulnerable crowds who appeared to be *sheep without a shepherd* (Matt. 9:36; Mark 6:34). He repeatedly ministered to the sick and oppressed with a heart of compassion (Mark 1:34; 6:56). He fed the hungry (John 6:10; Mark 8:6) and restored sight to the blind (Matt. 20:34; John 9:6-7). Even in the parable of the prodigal son, Jesus indicated that the father was *filled with compassion* when he ran to welcome his wayward son home (Luke 15:20). "True compassion is strength that is shared; it's God's agape love acted out on the objects of his love."[28] Jesus' compassion barometer was always focused on desperate whos.

My daughter Anna served as a short-term missionary in Bolivia one summer while she was in college. Before she left, she asked friends and family members to sew dresses and provide sweaters to take to the homeless children she anticipated she would meet there. This is an excerpt from one of her letters:

> While working on Saturday afternoons with a missionary who provides baths for street children, I was able to help literally clothe many of them. There are now dozens of little girls who have a dress to call their very own! And many little children now have a warm sweater to wear when they sleep at night. The missionary family who runs the project is building relationships with these children, and our desire is that they will hopefully have a relationship with Jesus one day, maybe even because of a dress or sweater that they were given by you. Jesus said, *"I needed clothes and you clothed me.... Truly, I tell you, whatever you did for one of the least of these brothers and sisters of mine, you did for me* (Matt. 25:36, 40).

Can you hear Jesus saying, *"I tell you, open your eyes and look at the fields! They are ripe for harvest"*? (John 4:35). He said that after showing indescribable compassion toward the Samaritan woman at the well. Her sinful lifestyle made her unworthy of a personal conversation with the King of Heaven, yet He offered her living water so she would never thirst again. Her life was transformed, and the lives of many other people in her town were transformed because she told them about Jesus, and they too believed on Him as *the Savior of the world* (John 4:41-42). He told His disciples to open their eyes so they could focus on those who were *ripe for harvest*. Listening to these same words ensures that our hearts are filled with His compassion, ready to recognize those who are desperate to be transformed by the Lord Jesus Christ. We are the workers in His harvest fields. We need to focus on the whos.

# Clear Focus Is Seeing the Whos through the Rearview Mirror

*Remember your leaders, who spoke the word of*
*God to you. Consider the outcome of their way of*
*life and imitate their faith.* Hebrews 13:7

One of the best ways for me to sharpen my focus on the whos in my life is to realize that I am a who to God. How humbling to realize that God has always focused on me from the time He *knit me together in my mother's womb* (Ps. 139:13). The fact that He takes notice of me at all is beyond my comprehension, not to mention that He wants to have a personal relationship with me. *How priceless is your unfailing love, O God!* (Ps. 36:7).

Brother Lawrence, a famous monk, the second half of his life in a French monastery in the 1600s, where he served as a cook. He dedicated his life to focusing his attention on God, although he came to realize that God's attention was actually focused on him:

> I consider myself as the most wretched of men, full of sores and corruption, and who has committed all sorts of crimes against His King. Touched with a sensible regret, I confess to Him all my wickedness, I ask His forgiveness, I abandon myself in His hands that He may do what He pleases with me. The King, full of mercy and goodness, very far from chastising me, embraces me with love, makes me eat at His table, serves me with His own hands, gives me the key of His treasures; He converses and delights Himself with me incessantly, in a thousand and a thousand ways, and treats me in all respects as His favorite. It is thus I consider myself from time to time in His holy presence.[29]

By looking through the rearview mirror of my life, I can see the many ways God has used others to rescue me and prepare me for usefulness in His kingdom. In a very real way, I believe Jesus said, *"Let us go over to the other side,"* to come and rescue me. The incarnation of Christ takes on a unique perspective when I see myself through the lens of the demon-possessed man. He was desperate, broken, and lost. Like him, I see this same Jesus coming to rescue me, and to do that, He used people who focused on me. In light of this, I have a renewed motivation to be used by God to rescue others. Wess Stafford encourages this kind of reflection:

> The first step on the journey forward is to pause and remember the "just a minute" moments in our own lives. Before eagerly reaching out to others, I may need to start by reaching back into myself. I cannot, after all, give to others what I do not have myself. I cannot pass on to others what I have not received. Precious people, whom we owe dearly for our lives, can be left in the dust, tiny images lost in the rearview mirrors of our lives. But if we will take the time for a brief glance backward, we might be surprised to see with new eyes some once-forgotten moments we would do well to recapture. Life-altering minutes. The spark of a dream that became a reality and shaped your life... or perhaps, sadly, one you have regretted every day since. We all have stories that explain who we are, why we do what we do—moments that, step by step, create and build our lives.[30]

We can all look backward in our lives and see key individuals God has used to focus on us. After reading the following examples from my life, I encourage you to take a break from reading this book. Take a trip down memory lane and celebrate the people God has used to focus on you. It will sharpen your focus on the whos God wants you to serve.

## Granddad

As a child, I had a great role model of someone who focused on whos—my grandfather, Rev. Richard Kindschi. I had the great privilege of attending his church most of my childhood. He was my hero, and as his oldest grandson, I wanted to grow up to be exactly like him. I still do.

I spent many hours with my grandfather in and around the church, and he often took me with him on pastoral visits. I watched and learned how selflessly he gave his life every day for the sheep in his flock. He was a wonderful, caring pastor who constantly demonstrated his love for his congregation in specific ways. Once I saw him pray with a widow in a hospital bed and then go right over to her house to fix her broken plumbing so she would not have to worry about it. There were countless similar examples. I am reminded of the Bible verse at the beginning of this section when I think of my grandfather. He often spoke the truth from God's Word into people's lives in natural and relevant ways they could understand. He was definitely worthy of imitation. That is the way he was—always taking care of someone else. After all, that is what a shepherd does.

Because I was so close to him, I often saw the difference he made in people's lives beyond what he did at the church. And I saw how much he was encouraged when people honored him and showed their appreciation. Sadly, I was also close enough to see how much it hurt him when people dishonored him and left the church over petty issues. In times like these, my grandfather taught me by his example what it meant to truly forgive people who hurt him. Somehow, he seemed to love them even more when they said unkind things to him or about him. He told me that he could forgive others because Jesus had forgiven him when he did things that hurt God. I am in Christian ministry today because of his influence. God also used many other Christian servants to shape me into a vessel fit for His service.

## Mom

A godly mother is one of life's greatest blessings. My mother probably does not realize it, but her life of dedication to the Lord Jesus is one of my greatest inspirations. I am reminded of 2 Timothy 3:15: *Since you were a child you have known the Holy Scriptures which are able to make you wise. And that wisdom leads to salvation through faith in Christ Jesus* (NCV). My mother constantly and naturally makes reference to God's Word in everyday conversations. When I became a Christian school educator, the concept of biblical integration was not new to me because my mother had clearly modeled it.

She is also a role model of how to focus on Who. Her focus on the Lord is exhibited by her prayerfulness in all things. Her first inclination is to pray about a matter instead of worry about it. She keeps her eyes fixed on Jesus as *the author and finisher of [her] faith* (Heb. 12:2 NKJV). She confidently quotes Romans 8:28: *We know that all things work together for good to those who love God, to those who are the called according to His purpose* (NKJV). She regularly and verbally rejoices in the Lord with overflowing joy over things that others take for granted. From this confidence in the Lord and overflowing joy, she serves others fervently. She gives constantly of herself, meeting the needs of others with selflessness and generosity. As I write this book, she is proofreading it and encouraging me. I am so privileged to be a special who that God entrusted to a wonderful Christian mother.

## Charles

As a deployed 19-year-old US Marine, I was far from home and, honestly, far from God. But God in His rich mercy focused His attention on me through another US Marine named Charles. He invited me to play soccer on a team that played in a weekend league off the base. I immediately noticed something different about him and the others on the team. They played competitively, but throughout the game, they verbally encouraged one another, the referees, and the opposing team's players. After several games, I asked questions about their different attitudes and behavior.

Instead of answering my questions, Charles asked me a question: "Do you ever feel like God is disappointed with you?"

I answered almost without thinking. "All the time," I said.

Charles then sketched a picture of how Jesus came to rescue me when there was no way that I could ever measure up to God's righteous standards. (He used the Navigator's Bridge to Life Illustration.)[31] In that moment, I realized I was the who Jesus came to save, and I surrendered my life to Him. Charles mentored me for the next two years, meeting with me every week to help me grow in my Christian faith. He poured his time, energy, and resources into my life, equipping me for a future ministry in

Christian education that I could not have possibly imagined at the time. When I remember Charles, I think of Colossians 2:6-7: *And now, just as you accepted Christ Jesus as your Lord, you must continue to follow him. Let your roots grow down into him, and let your lives be built on him. Then your faith will grow strong in the truth you were taught, and you will overflow with thankfulness* (NLT).

## Melanie

*Then the LORD God said, "It is not good for the man to be alone. I will make a helper who is just right for him"* (Gen. 2:18 NLT). When God wanted me to know that I was a very special who, He gave me Melanie to be my wife, companion, and best friend. I often contemplate how my life might have turned out if she had not been alongside me for the past thirty years to encourage me, believe in me, and inspire me to be all that God designed me to be. She was actually the missionary God used to draw me closer to Him. When we first met, I realized she had a deep fellowship with God that I did not have. She was focused on Who, and I was focused on what. Her love for Jesus was contagious, and I realized I needed to focus on Him as well. As I did, my love for Him grew as well as my love for her.

Melanie is others-focused. Anyone who knows her recognizes that she constantly gives herself away in service to others. She not only supplies me with a steady stream of encouragement that fuels my ability to serve others, but she also invests herself joyfully in the lives of our children, family members, and all the other whos God places in her path, enabling them to reach their full potential. My favorite thing about Melanie is her deep compassion for others. She reminds me of Jesus who always gave of Himself to meet the desperate needs of those who were in pain. This is love—this is focusing on whos. As I think about my precious wife, I am reminded of Proverbs 31:28-29: *Her children arise and call her blessed; her husband also, and he praises her: "Many women do noble things, but you surpass them all."*

Okay. Now it is your turn to look into the rearview mirror of your life to see God's loving provision and the whos He has used to focus on you.

# Clear Focus Is Obtained When We Serve with the Right Motivation

*We ought not to be weary of doing little things for the love*
*of God, who regards not the greatness of the work, but the*
*love with which it is performed.* Brother Lawrence[32]

The way we use the word *ministry* in our Christian circles puzzles me sometimes. Ministry seems to have taken on a meaning that is elevated beyond what was originally intended. Of course we use it to indicate and honor the calling to vocational Christian service for people such as pastors, missionaries, and teachers. We also refer to our Christian organizations as ministries. There is a measure of accuracy in how we use the word, but I wonder if we have missed the biblical meaning of ministry. What would happen if we used the biblical terminology of a servant to describe our Christian organizations and ourselves? The words used in Scripture are serve (*diakoneo*) or servant (*doulos*).[33]

Sometimes we approach God from our misguided definition of ministry as if He owes us something for our service. Instead of understanding the privilege we have been granted to serve Him, we can miss the relational value afforded us through this arrangement. Richard Pratt says,

> A servant's look is not an occasional glance at God but an intense gaze at Him.... We often treat prayer like a spiritual shopping list. We walk into God's general store, give a perfunctory nod in His direction and then proceed to the real reason we came—the grocery list. We spend the bulk of our time listing one request after another, and God Himself takes second place. In fact, this habit of ignoring God suggests that we would prefer to find Him absent from the store so we would not have to bother with Him at all. How easy it is to forget that we are dealing with a divine Person, not a heavenly mail-order catalog. When we focus too much on what we need, we are bound to neglect the One whom we need.[34]

To combat this kind of selfish-servant mentality with an obsessive focus on whats, I sometimes imagine myself entering a great banquet hall for a formal meal. At the head of the table sits King Jesus in all His glory. All around the table are seated His invited guests—students, teachers, and parents from our Christian schools. The king's attention is focused on them, and it is easy to see that they are the supreme joy of His heart. He has called me—not to be seated at the table—but to serve Him and to serve His invited guests as a waiter at His table. My attention is to be focused on Him and His invited guests—not on myself.

I am filled with humble gratitude that He would allow me to serve Him at all, in any capacity. Because of my sins, I should be locked away in His dungeon below the banquet hall. But because of His great mercy, He allowed me to sit at His table for a while, and now He grants me the privilege to serve at His table, representing Him to His guests. I also have the wonderful opportunity to serve alongside other servants, all of us working together to ensure the king's banquet meets with His approval and pleasure. It is an honor to be called to serve, and I am overwhelmed with joy that He allows me to serve these particular guests at His banquet table. Envision this scene as you read Psalm 123:1-2:

> *I lift my eyes to you, O God, enthroned in heaven. We keep looking to the LORD our God for his mercy, just as servants keep their eyes on their master, as a slave girl watches her mistress for the slightest signal.* (NLT)

The servant girl is *watching for the slightest signal.* That is remarkable. I long to develop that kind of clear focus as a servant—to be so intent on pleasing the Master that I am able to catch His slightest glance toward one of His guests so I can meet one of their needs in His name. That is the essence of focusing on Who.

Jesus had that kind of clear focus when it came to serving. He said, *"The Son of Man did not come to be served, but to serve, and to give his life as a ransom for many"* (Mark 10:45). He demonstrated His heart for serving when He washed His disciples' feet at the Last Supper and encouraged them to follow His example (John 13:1-17). Paul reminds us of this in Philippians 2:3-7:

*When you do things, do not let selfishness or pride be your guide. Instead, be humble and give more honor to others than to yourselves. Do not be interested only in your own life, but be interested in the lives of others. In your lives you must think and act like Christ Jesus. Christ himself was like God in everything. But he did not think that being equal with God was something to be used for his own benefit. But he gave up his place with God and made himself nothing. He was born as a man and became like a servant.* (NCV)

Being a servant in Christian ministry is not always easy. Sometimes the Master asks us to do difficult things. In John 2:5, Mary, the mother of Jesus, told the servants at the wedding of Cana, *"Do whatever he tells you to do"* (NCV). Jesus could have asked the servants to do almost anything, but He simply asked them to fill six stone water pots with water. While this was likely a difficult task—each pot held thirty gallons of water—it was something they were capable of doing. This helps me. I take comfort in knowing that Jesus will never ask me to do something I am not able to do. One of the servants was asked to do something a bit more difficult—probably outside of his comfort zone. He had to take some of the water and give it to the master of the feast. Again, it was something he could do, but it could have produced an embarrassing situation. But he did exactly what Jesus told him to do. As a result, he and the other servants were granted a front-row seat to Jesus' first miracle—turning the water into wine.

While serving is a great honor, it is not always enjoyable. Sometimes the cost of serving the Lord results in mistreatment or even abuse. This happened to many of the prophets, disciples, and to Jesus Himself. God does not promise that serving Him will be easy. In fact, Jesus said, *"Whoever wants to be my disciple must deny themselves and take up their cross and follow me"* (Matt. 16:24). He illustrated this in a parable:

*A man planted a vineyard and leased it to some farmers. Then he went away for a long time. When it was time for the grapes to be picked, he sent a servant to the farmers to get some of the grapes. But they beat the servant and sent him away empty-handed. Then he sent another servant. They beat this servant also, and showed no respect for him, and sent him away empty-handed. So the man sent a third servant. The farmers wounded him and threw him out. The owner of the vineyard said, "What will I do now? I will send my son whom I love. Maybe they will respect him." But when the farmers saw the son, they said to each other, "This son will inherit the vineyard. If we kill him, it will be ours." So the farmers threw the son out of the vineyard and killed him.*

*[Jesus asked,] "What will the owner of this vineyard do to them? He will come and kill those farmers and will give the vineyard to other farmers." When the people heard this story, they said, "Let this never happen!" But Jesus looked at them and said, "Then what does this verse mean: 'The stone that the builders rejected became the cornerstone'? Everyone who falls on that stone will be broken, and the person on whom it falls, that person will be crushed!"* (Luke 20:9-18 NCV)

In this parable, Jesus illustrated the kindness of God (the vineyard owner) to send servants (prophets) before Him. But they were ignored, abused, and wounded. Even the son himself was rejected and killed. While the servants are not the focus of the parable, their role is intriguing. They were agents of God's extravagant patience toward those who did not deserve His mercy. As a result, they were mistreated and even killed.

In our role as servants in Christian education, we may sometimes feel ignored, abused, wounded, or rejected. Could it be that we are God's agents of extravagant patience toward our students, their parents, or our colleagues? His loving mercy prompts Him to send us to them. And how many of His servants have we ignored, abused, wounded, or rejected? Perhaps this parable can remind us to be more patient ourselves when we are the servants.

Someone once asked Lorne Sanny, the president of the Navigators, how to know whether he was truly being a servant. Sanny said, "By the way you react when people treat you like one."[35] We do not deserve to have the role of servant—it is a gift of grace. Maintaining a humble perspective on why God has chosen us to serve Him is essential; otherwise, we will not be able to serve with the right motivation. When St. Francis of Assisi was asked why people followed him, he said,

> It is because the eyes of the Most High have willed it so. He continually watches the good and the wicked, and as His most holy eyes have not found among sinners any smaller man, nor any more insufficient and sinful, therefore He has chosen me to accomplish the marvelous work which God has undertaken; He chose me because He could find none more worthless, and He wished to confound the nobility and grandeur, the strength, the beauty and the learning of this world.[36]

No doubt, St. Francis had this passage of Scripture in mind:

> *Remember, dear brothers and sisters, that few of you were wise in the world's eyes or powerful or wealthy when God called you. Instead, God chose things the world considers foolish in order to shame those who think they are wise. And he chose things that are powerless to shame those who are powerful. God chose things despised by the world, things counted as nothing at all, and used them to bring to nothing what the world considers important. As a result, no one can ever boast in the presence of God.* (1 Cor. 1:26-29 NLT)

The key role of a servant is to represent his master. Once we realize that we have been chosen to serve—not because of our worthiness, but because of His mercy—then we can be humble ambassadors for Christ. Because His motivation is love, ours must be love as well. In fact, if love is not our motivation, it does not matter how gifted or talented we may be (1 Cor. 13:1-3).

Serving with the right motivation is essential for clear focus. Because we serve such a gracious and loving God, it is easy to lose our perspective and develop a sense of entitlement. We can become haughty or arrogant, expecting others to treat us with distinctive honor because of our position in the kingdom. But Jesus demonstrated perfectly how we are to serve—although He was equal with God, He *took the humble position of a slave* to serve us, taking our place on the cross (Phil. 2:6-8 NLT).

Only with the humble love of Christ can we truly serve others.

I Wonder
by Ruth Harms Calkin

You know, Lord, how I serve you
With great emotional fervor
In the limelight.
You know how eagerly I speak for you
At a women's club.
You know how I effervesce when I promote
A fellowship group.
You know my genuine enthusiasm
At a Bible study.
But how would I react, I wonder,
If you pointed to a basin of water
And you asked me to wash the calloused feet
Of a bent and wrinkled old woman
Day after day
Month after month
In a room where nobody saw
And nobody knew. [37]

# Clear Focus Is Evidenced by Joy

*Those who look to him for help will be radiant with joy; no
shadow of shame will darken their faces.* Psalm 34:5 (NLT)

When I speak with Christian school educators, I like to ask them, "What is
your greatest joy and what is your greatest challenge in ministry?" Almost
without fail, their answer to the first part of the question begins with a
who. They describe for me, in some detail, how a particular student or
colleague brings them joy, especially when spiritual growth is in clear focus
within the relationship. Often their faces light up with excitement as they
recount for me the specifics of a student who came to Christ, a coworker
who is an encouragement, or an alumnus who is serving the Lord in some
capacity.

When I bring up the second part of the question—their greatest
challenge in ministry—the conversation typically becomes less enjoyable.
Their countenance usually changes to reflect their weariness or angst,
and they begin to describe a difficult set of circumstances that is almost
always centered on a what. The range of challenges tends to span from
their workload (the frenetic "rowing") to financial obstacles or personal
struggles. In answering this two-part question, they often realize the
second part is preventing them from experiencing more of the first part.
They seem to be controlled by the tyranny of the urgent—an endless list
of whats that prevents them from spending quality time with whos.

Sometimes the challenge they share is personified in a difficult who.
In such cases, their focus is not set on seeing this who with eyes of faith
through the lens of Jesus' mercy and compassion. Usually, this who
(student, coworker, parent, or leader) has become a source of anger, pain,
confusion, or bitterness. On more than one occasion, Christian school
educators have said they would love their ministry if it were not for a
particular person who makes their life miserable.

Let me pause to comment on that perspective. Do we actually expect
to serve Jesus Christ without someone making our life miserable? Even a
cursory reading of the New Testament will reveal numerous individuals
who seemed to work diligently to make Jesus and His disciples miserable.
Jesus was mercilessly killed for what He taught, and His followers who

established the early church often paid a serious price for their commitment to the gospel. Oddly enough, most of their opposition came from religious people. Even today, many suffer greatly at the hand of sinners who rage against the gospel of Jesus Christ and His servants. Clay Werner says,

> One look at Jesus hanging on the cross will teach you that if you make a conscious decision to deeply and sacrificially love sinners, it's going to hurt something awful. I mean really, really, really bad. When the tears from the pain and agony and frustration and exhaustion of ministry cover the eyes of your heart, you begin to lose sight of the incredible power and amazing hope that the gospel of Jesus Christ gives you. One look at Jesus will also teach you that if God loved us even to the point of death on a cross, he'll provide strength to endure and hope to persevere through the incredible and humanly impossible calling of loving fellow sinners.[38]

In the midst of extreme suffering on the cross inflicted by difficult whos, Jesus still had joy because He knew what He was accomplishing for us (Heb. 12:2). He loved us so deeply that even while He was being tortured and put to death, He prayed, *"Father forgive them, for they do not know what they are doing"* (Luke 23:34). We will face difficult people in our ministries—some whose own lives are so broken that they do not know how to love and forgive. We will face opposition, unfair treatment, and perhaps persecution for the sake of Christ. But what we need to do is *think of all the hostility he endured from sinful people; then [we] won't become weary and give up* (Heb. 12:3 NLT).

Whether our greatest challenge is an unpleasant what or a difficult who, the result is the same: stolen joy in ministry. Stolen joy is like removing the battery out of our smart phones or computers. All that potential to communicate and provide valuable information is crippled without the power source. Nehemiah said, *"The joy of the LORD is your strength"* (Neh. 8:10). When our ministry in Christian education is filled with the joy of the Lord, we will have His strength to "row" to the destination He has chosen for us. This joy comes from keeping our focus on Him, receiving

His joy, and then sharing it with others. This kind of joy is an accelerator of other spiritual fruit. Michael Zigarelli says,

> From a biblical point of view, we can define joy as "having a daily spirit of rejoicing through all circumstances." It is more than inner contentment, more than gladness, more than overall satisfaction with life. Rather, joy is a spirit of celebrating life, of delighting in all that God has bestowed on us. In combination with gratitude and God-centeredness, joyful living is a hallmark that sets apart high-virtue Christians from average-virtue Christians... for high-virtue Christians, their joy spawns other virtues.[39]

We named our youngest child Rebecca Joy. Even as a newborn baby, she brought joy to our hearts and to everyone around her. She still does. I have often pondered the source of her joy, beyond the fact that it is a fruit of the Holy Spirit. Like many of us, she is not always happy with her circumstances. In fact, she has endured some serious challenges along the way. Yet she still has a deep, abiding joy that is contagious. As I wrote this chapter, I realized that the source of her joy is connected to her compassion for others—a focus on the whos in her life. She has a unique way of identifying with the needs of others, meeting those needs (often through her own sacrifice), then transferring her joy to them in the process. She is the one who goes out of her way to help a homeless person, to support a poor child through Compassion International, to sing to a crying baby, or to stay with a friend through the night at the hospital. In effect, she strengthens others with the strength she has received from her joy in the Lord.

We all can experience joy even when burdensome circumstances or people attempt to distract our focus. Our role model is our Lord Jesus who endured the cross—a most difficult circumstance at the hand of most difficult people—with joy (Heb. 12:2). The God of hope will fill us with all joy and peace, as we trust in Him, by the power of the Holy Spirit (Rom. 15:13). This allows us to focus on Him instead of the circumstances or the problems we may face in ministry. James wrote, *when troubles come your way, consider it an opportunity for great joy* (James 1:2 NLT). This is because our faith and endurance in ministry become stronger as we persevere through our struggles.

We cannot allow our joy to be stolen by the enemy, by negative circumstances, or by problematic people. We must renew our focus on Who (and who); then we will see our joy and strength in ministry return. Even the angels of God have joy over one sinner who repents (Luke 15:10). Consider Paul's joy over the new believers in Thessalonica: *For what is our hope or joy or crown of boasting before our Lord Jesus at his coming? Is it not you? For you are our glory and joy* (1 Thess. 2:19-20 ESV). One of my favorite Bible verses is 3 John 4: *I have no greater joy than to hear that my children are walking in the truth.*

What is your greatest joy in Christian school ministry? Are difficult whats or whos stealing your joy? If so, redirect your focus to the true source of your joy—Jesus Christ. He wants to give us His joy so that our joy may be complete (John 15:11; 17:13). Then we will be able to clearly focus on the whos He has brought into our lives and have even more joy as we see them learn to walk in the truth.

# Clear Focus Prioritizes What in Order to Serve Who

pri·or·i·ty (prī'ôrədē)—*a thing that is regarded
as more important than another.*[40]

Everyone in the room was stunned. Usually, a servant washed everyone's feet before the meal. But this was Mary—Martha and Lazarus's younger sister. She did not have a basin of water or a towel. Instead, she carried her most valuable possession—an alabaster jar of expensive perfume (Matt. 26:6-13; Mark 14:1-9; John 12:1-8). Everyone knew of Mary's devotion to Jesus whenever He came to Bethany. With raptured attention, she loved to sit at Jesus' feet and listen to Him teach. He had commended her for this on an earlier occasion and reproved her sister Martha for being distracted with so many other things (Luke 10:38-42). They had gathered once again for a dinner to honor Jesus before the Passover. Lazarus reclined at the table with Jesus. No one could get over the fact that Jesus had brought him back to life after he had been buried in a tomb for four days earlier that year. How wonderful to have Jesus back with all of them again!

Suddenly, a collective gasp rippled through the room as Mary did the unthinkable—she broke the seal on the alabaster jar and poured the perfume on Jesus' hair and feet, anointing Him with reverence and worship. Many must have thought, *How could she do it?* That treasure possibly represented her life's savings, or perhaps it was an heirloom passed down to her—worth a full year's wages. Judas Iscariot was especially offended. He mentioned that it could have been sold—instead of "wasted"—and the money given to the poor. (He was actually a thief who only wanted the money for himself.) But Jesus defended Mary and told everyone to leave her alone because she was preparing His body for burial.

As the fragrance of her extravagant offering filled the room, Mary once again sat at Jesus' feet, but this time, she wiped His feet with her hair. Perhaps the familiar words of Isaiah came to her mind: *How beautiful ... are the feet of those who bring good news* (Isa. 52:7). Jesus valued Mary's sacrificial focus on Him. He said that whenever the gospel is preached throughout the world, the beautiful thing she had done would be remembered (Matt. 26:13).

In this story, we are stunned by the contrast between Mary's focus on Who and the disciples' focus on what. Mary gave everything she had, both materially and humanly, because she adored her Lord and Savior. She placed a higher priority on Jesus than on physical treasure. Sadly, the disciples were fixated on the expensive what and felt that it was being wasted. In fact, the Bible says they were "indignant" (Matt. 26:8)—offended by Mary's decision to prioritize Who over what. This illustrates how easily we become distracted in our focus in ministry. Thankfully, Jesus came to her defense and validated her focus on Who. "There is something inexpressibly sad, yet so patient, gentle, and tender in Christ's 'Let her alone.' Surely, never could there be waste in ministry of love to Him!"[41]

Most Christian school faculty, staff, and leaders answered the call of Christian education because they recognized the opportunity to impact the next generation for Jesus Christ—the whos. Many serve because they believe that the mantra of Christian education is found in Psalm 78:4-7:

> *We will tell the next generation the praiseworthy deeds of the LORD, his power, and the wonders he has done… so the next generation would know them, even the children yet to be born, and they in turn would tell their children. Then they would put their trust in God and would not forget his deeds but would keep his commands.*

I have attended large Christian school gatherings where this passage of Scripture produces a rousing applause by Christian school educators. By investing their lives in the next generation through the evangelism and discipleship that occurs in Christian schools, they believe they are helping to fulfill the Great Commission of Jesus Christ. But something seems to happen to them over time, squelching their enthusiasm and dulling their passion.

What begins to replace who.

Many whats can distract us in Christian school ministry. Many of them are good whats. Curriculum, lesson plans, assignments, e-mails, meetings, strategic plans, budgets, buildings, extracurricular activities, and events are all essential whats in a Christian school. They are like the boat and the oars in Jesus' trip to the other side—necessary resources to transport Him to His next ministry assignment. Christian schools also need a host of resources to effectively accomplish their mission. But when these whats become the focus, taking priority over the whos, we become distracted and fruitless. We construct boat-building factories and schools of rowing, but lives are not changed because there is no who in our ministry. We shift our focus to the value of potential ministry resources as the disciples did with the alabaster jar, instead of realizing that the most valuable thing in our Christian schools is our Lord Jesus and the people He has called us to serve.

Consider the way Jesus prioritized the whats in order to serve the whos in His ministry. He often made use of common objects or resources, but He always used them as tools that enabled Him to bring His message of hope to mankind: what always served who.

- The Manger. Jesus' first resource was a common manger where cattle were fed (Luke 2:16). The manger still remains a powerful symbol around the world today, testifying of the incarnation of Christ. Emmanuel—God with us, taking on the humble form of a human baby, born in ignoble circumstances, born to *save his people from their sins* (Matt. 1:21).
- Boats. Jesus seemed to love boats. But He always used boats as a means to provide people with truth, hope, healing, and salvation (Luke 5:3; Mark 4:1-5:43; 8:31-37).
- Fish and Bread. Jesus often used these two common resources to provide miraculously for those who followed Him (Matt. 14:13-21; John 21:6). He also used them metaphorically to show that people were His primary focus: *"I will make you fishers of men"* (Matt. 4:19); *"I am the bread of life"* (John 6:35); *"This is my body given for you"* (Luke 22:19).
- Water. He turned it into wine (John 2:9), He promised living water (John 4:14), He was baptized in it (Matt. 3:16), He calmed it (Mark 4:39), He walked on it (Matt. 14:25), and He washed feet with it (John 13:5). In every instance, He used water to meet the needs of one or more whos.
- The Cross and Tomb. Jesus transformed the cross (a cruel instrument of execution) and its cold, lifeless result (the tomb)

into the ultimate resources of heaven for everyone who calls on the name of Jesus. He canceled the record of the charges against us and took it away by nailing it to the cross (Col. 2:14), and He conquered death, hell, and the grave! *He is not here; he has risen, just as he said* (Matt. 28:6). He did this so that we could be dead to our sin and raised to live a new life with Him (Rom. 6:5-14).

Jesus always prioritized whats to meet the needs of whos. Certainly, He faced as many distractions in His ministry as we do, but He kept His focus on His heavenly Father and on those He came to save. Yes, we should take into account the various conditions, circumstances, and resources necessary to accomplish what God has called us to do. The whats are vital considerations. But they cannot become the focal point. In the story about Rowing to the Other Side Ministries, an obsessive fixation with the whats became the purpose for the ministry, which thrived for quite some time without a single who. Focusing on the whos allows us to fill each day in our ministry with the extraordinary, not the mundane. We focus on the eternal instead of the temporal. Therefore, we must regularly assess our priorities in ministry to ensure they are focused on whos.

When my daughter Anna's boyfriend, Kevin, (now my son-in-law), asked to meet with me after about a year of dating her, I knew my life was about to change. After some nervous conversation about college and NFL football, Kevin said he wanted to ask me something. I held my breath and tried to focus. Right—focus! He told me how much he loved Anna and how they wanted to take their relationship to the next level.

Courtship.

Whew! I had expected him to ask me for her hand in marriage (which he did about a year later). I was impressed with Kevin's definition of courtship and how it would involve a more serious commitment in their relationship to explore the potential for marriage. I had only one question for him. "How will you protect Anna's reputation and encourage her spiritual growth during this time of courtship?" He had come well prepared for such a question, and he pulled out a list from his pocket of commitments he and Anna had made to one another (with the help of a mentor) to ensure their relationship would please the Lord and foster their spiritual growth. The entire list was dedicated to placing a priority in their relationship to focus on Who (and who). I do not recall a single what in the list. Their happy marriage is an ongoing testimony to the clear focus that comes when we prioritize what in order to serve who.

# Clear Focus Is Developed with Heat and Pressure

*The crucible is for silver, and the furnace is for gold,*
*and the LORD tests hearts.* Proverbs 17:3 (ESV)

I enjoy watching a television program called *How It's Made* on the Science Channel. The show, which debuted in 2001, takes viewers behind the scenes in different factories to reveal the process for making hundreds of everyday items from aluminum foil to airplanes and almost anything in between. Occasionally, the Science Channel will run a weekend-long marathon of *How It's Made* episodes. My wife and daughters cannot understand why my son and I want to camp out in the living room and watch every single one. They are fascinating.

Watching this show over the years, I have learned that almost every product requires two common elements: extreme heat and pressure. The workers interviewed in the various factories also seem to enjoy applying the extreme heat and pressure because they know those elements allow them to make their product. I often joke that I could go out in my backyard, dig up a big pile of dirt, apply extreme amounts of heat and pressure and out would pop a new car. Obviously, it is not that simple, but if you think about it, every component necessary to assemble a car originates from elements mined out of the ground and then subjected to heat and pressure. That is true for everything we see around us—even human beings are made out of clay (Gen. 2:7). So what about the heat and pressure for us?

Paul described the kind of heat and pressure he experienced in his ministry: *We are hard pressed on every side, but not crushed; perplexed, but not in despair; persecuted, but not abandoned; struck down, but not destroyed* (2 Cor. 4:8-9). Paul's perseverance resulted from his dependence on the all-surpassing power of God. At the end of chapter four, he said that he did not focus on his *light and momentary troubles.* Instead, he fixed his gaze on things that cannot be seen that will last forever (2 Cor. 4:17-18 NIV).

In Romans 5:3-5, Paul encourages us to rejoice in our sufferings or troubles, knowing that they produce perseverance, which produces character, which produces hope. The Greek word Paul used for *perseverance* is *humomone* defined as "the spirit which meets things [directly] forward and overcomes them."[42] Enduring our trials and overcoming our tribulations (our heat and pressure) build character in our lives and ministries. *Character, (dokime)*, is the word used to describe metal that has passed through fire so everything impure has been purged out of it. Peter had *dokime* in mind when he wrote:

> *So be truly glad. There is wonderful joy ahead, even though you have to endure many trials for a little while. These trials will show that your faith is genuine. It is being tested as fire tests and purifies gold—though your faith is far more precious than mere gold. So when your faith remains strong through many trials, it will bring you much praise and glory and honor on the day when Jesus Christ is revealed to the whole world.* (1 Peter 1:6-7 NLT)

So heat and pressure help us develop a clear focus in ministry. None of us want to volunteer to go through seasons of difficulty or suffering, but whenever we find ourselves in those seasons, we can be assured that God is forging our character to be stronger in life and ministry. "When affliction is met with fortitude, out of the battle a man emerges stronger, and purer, and better, and nearer to God."[43] This kind of character produces hope—a confident expectation that cannot be disappointed. It actually becomes *an anchor for the soul, firm and secure* (Heb. 6:19). Matthew Henry says,

> We are in this world as a ship at sea, tossed up and down, and in danger of being cast away. We need an anchor to keep us sure and steady. Gospel hope is our anchor, sure and steadfast, that has taken hold upon Christ; he is the anchor-hold of the believer's hope.[44]

Sometimes, the heat and pressure we experience in our lives and ministry are the result of the loving correction and discipline of the Lord. While this can be painful, it produces *a harvest of righteousness and peace for those who have been trained by it* (Heb. 12:11).

Years ago, when I was an inexperienced elementary principal, a teacher came to my office with a small boy who had evidently caused some trouble in her classroom. She said, "I need for you to put the fear of God in this young man!" With that declaration, she walked away, leaving the student standing in the doorway of my office. I asked him to take a seat across from my desk while I considered what to do. I can still see his little feet swinging under the adult-sized chair in which he sat, his fear-filled eyes welling up with tears. (I am honestly not sure which of us was more afraid!)

"So you must have really upset your teacher, huh?" I asked.

He looked down and said nervously, "Yes sir."

Having three small children of my own at that time, I wanted to go over to him, hug him, and tell him it would be okay, but I knew that the role I had been assigned by the teacher was to "put the fear of God" in him. As I prayed silently, the Holy Spirit brought Hebrews 12:11 to my mind. This was a training opportunity for the boy, and if I handled it correctly, he could experience a *harvest of righteousness and peace* as a result.

It is not the fear of God that brings us to repentance.

It is His kindness (Rom. 2:4).

Now I knew what to do. But how?

Again, the Holy Spirit reminded me of another verse regarding correction—Galatians 6:1: *Brothers and sisters, if someone is caught in a sin, you who live by the Spirit should restore that person gently. But watch yourselves, or you also may be tempted.* My goal for this student was restoration—gentle restoration of his relationship with his teacher. Suddenly, the second part of the verse stung me like a bee. *But watch yourselves, or you also may be tempted.* I then knew what I needed to do. I asked the young man if he would mind if I made a telephone call. He seemed visibly relieved that my attention was being drawn away from him. I picked up the telephone receiver and dialed my home number.

"Melanie, I'm calling to ask you to forgive me," I said humbly. "I was wrong for speaking disrespectfully to you this morning. I'm so sorry. Will you please forgive me?"

Only an hour earlier, when I was leaving home, I had lost my patience with my wife, and I had said some unkind, hurtful things to her. I was the one who needed to be marched to the principal's office to have the "fear of God" put in me. But in His own gentle way, God had disciplined me by the power of His Spirit and His Word to produce a *harvest of righteousness and peace* in my own life and marriage. My loving and gracious wife assured me that she had already forgiven me and added that she was praying for me to have a good day at school. Of course, she did not know I was in the middle of a disciplinary meeting with a student.

I turned my attention back to the boy who looked up at me with a bewildered expresssion. I told him that I too had been disrespectful that morning and needed to apologize for the things I had said. I asked him if he thought he could do the same thing with his teacher. He said he could, so I sent him back to his classroom.

At the end of the day, the teacher returned to my office and asked to meet with me. I thought perhaps she might not have appreciated my inability to adequately "put the fear of God" in her student, so I braced myself for criticism. Instead, she thanked me for meeting with the student and apologized for the way she had handled the situation in her frustration. Then she asked me, "What did you say to him? He was so sorry when he returned to class, and he behaved perfectly the rest of the day."

I replied, "I really didn't say anything to him. I repented of my own sin, and he saw how he could do the same."

Heat and pressure are significant in our Christian life and ministry. We actually need them to be shaped into a *vessel of honor* fit for God's service (Rom. 9:21 NKJV). Few, if any, of us want to sign up for more heat and pressure, but when we experience them under the sovereign care of God, we can learn to appreciate the eternal benefits that come as a result.

> *Pure gold put in the fire comes out of it proved pure; genuine faith put through this suffering comes out proved genuine. When Jesus wraps this all up, it's your faith, not your gold, that God will have on display as evidence of his victory.* (1 Peter 1:7 MSG)

# Clear Focus Is Unwavering in Storms and Battles

*But Stephen, full of the Holy Spirit, hardly noticed—*
*he only had eyes for God, whom he saw in all his glory*
*with Jesus standing at his side.* Acts 7:55 (MSG)

Storms and battles are scary. I have experienced both, and they contain similarities. They often surprise us with shock and awe, attacking us from our blind side. They usually produce debilitating fear along with physical or emotional pain. They may force us to go places we would not otherwise go. And when they are relentless, they can make us want to give up, especially after we have exhausted all our resources combating them. We would not choose to go through storms and battles, but when we do, they have a way of clarifying for us what is truly important. They perfect our focus.

The disciples battled a storm that evening on the way to the other side of the Sea of Galilee. They were caught by surprise, afraid for their lives, tossed by the wind and waves, attacked by evil, and ready to give up hope. In times like these, we usually run to Jesus—and the disciples did. Their focus was not what it should have been, but He still intervened and said, *"Peace, be still"* (Mark 4:39 NKJV). Their focus probably became quite clear in that moment!

We should not be surprised that Christian school ministry has its share of storms and battles. We live in a fallen world filled with circumstances that rise up like storms in our lives. We have an enemy who does not want us to succeed in providing our students with a Christ-centered, biblically based education. *We are not fighting against flesh-and-blood enemies, but against evil rulers and authorities of the unseen world, against mighty powers in this dark world, and against evil spirits in the heavenly places* (Eph. 6:12 NLT). We will be attacked at every turn.

During storms and battles, how do we keep an unwavering, clear focus?

We keep our eyes on Jesus and on one another.

That advice sounds so simple. We believe it and advise others to follow it when they are fighting some monstrous storm or battle. But for some reason, whenever we find ourselves in one of these situations, we tend to act in a self-preserving manner. We become annoyed, upset, and even angry as the ship of our life or ministry is tossed about in tumultuous waves. We become defensive, offended, and bitter when the battle lines cross into our personal territory. Where is our focus? On ourselves.

My daughter Anna is a first-year teacher in a Christian school. She has already endured her fair share of storms and battles. But despite the challenging circumstances and difficult people she has faced along her journey, she shared this with her friends and family:

> Even in the darkest of times, the light of Jesus shines through. In the midst of extreme hardship and division in my classroom this week, I was able to lead one of my students to Jesus after school today. I know now, I am exactly where I am supposed to be.

There it is! Her focus became crystal clear as she endured the storm. On the other side, there was a who waiting to meet Jesus. Perhaps the storm and the battle she fought was an attempt by the enemy to keep this precious child, for whom Christ died, from receiving the gospel. Or maybe it was only another day in this sin-infested world that often brings out the worst in all of us. Either way, I am so grateful for her unwavering commitment to persevere because she had her eyes turned toward Jesus in the darkest of times to see His light shining. *In him there was life, and that life was the light of all people. The Light shines in the darkness, and the darkness has not overpowered it* (John 1:4 NCV). Billy Graham reminds us to find our peace in Christ during the storms of life:

> The storm was raging. The sea was beating against the rocks in huge, dashing waves. The lightning was flashing, the thunder was roaring, the wind was blowing; but the little bird was asleep in the crevice of the rock, its head serenely under its wing, sound asleep. That is peace: to be able to rest serenely in the storm! In Christ we are relaxed and at peace in the midst of the confusions, bewilderments, and perplexities of this life. The storm rages, but our hearts are at rest. We have found peace—at last![45]

# Clear Focus Facilitates Conflict Resolution

*Blessed are the peacemakers, for they will be
called children of God.* Matthew 5:9

Peace in a relationship is one of the most enjoyable things in life. Can you imagine what our lives would be like without conflict? The thought alone causes us to take a deep sigh of relief. But in reality, how often is that true in our lives? Practically never. There always seems to be someone, somewhere who does not agree with us or does not want what we want.

Why is it so difficult to get along with each other?

Conflict is inevitable—especially in ministry situations. Clay Warner says, "Ministry includes other people. Other people have their own desires, their own struggles, their own opinions, their own gifts, and their own plans."[46] Most of the time, conflict in ministry relationships is the personification of selfishness. *Do you know where your fights and arguments come from? They come from the selfish desires that war within you. You want things, but you do not have them* (James 4:1-2 NCV). Sometimes conflict is the result either of unwillingness to submit to authority or of someone in authority *lording it over* another person (1 Peter 5:3). Conflict can be the outcome of poor communication, misunderstanding, or misbehavior. But whatever the cause, we probably would all agree that conflict is miserable, creating emotional pain and mental anxiety and causing us to lose our focus on the whos.

Two natural responses to conflict are common: fight or flight—a concept initially coined by Harvard Professor Walter Bradford Cannon in 1915 after conducting research related to emotional response caused by pain, hunger, fear, and rage.[47] Some people are inclined to avoid conflict at any cost, even if it means that they become doormats for others to step on. They run at the first sign of conflict and bury their emotional pain and mental anxiety, which can result in unforgiveness, bitterness, and division. These people generally say something like, "I just decided to let that go," which may mean they have started stacking up bricks to build a wall in the relationship to protect themselves. Eventually, this wall becomes so high that it prevents effective communication in the relationship, which prompts the person to add more bricks. Other people are inclined to fight for what they want. They will use almost any means available (strong words, bullying tactics, or manipulating circumstances) to convince others that they are right. When opposed, they may become indignant and offended, creating a deep chasm of separation they use to punish others for their unwillingness to yield to their desires.

Neither of these responses generates peace in the relationship. Both are focused on a what (namely what we want or deserve) instead of a who. Interestingly, both approaches stem from people believing that they are entirely right and others are entirely wrong. In this context, the only solution to the conflict is for either of the parties to change their mind so peace can be restored. For some people, peacemaking is defined as caving in to the pressure of division (either from the separating wall or the dividing chasm) and compromising—essentially giving other people what they want in order to restore harmony.

This is not peacemaking; it is bargaining.

It does not address the source of conflict. The conflict is temporarily swept under the proverbial rug until it reappears in the next conflict.

Both fight and flight approaches of handling conflict can be seen across a broad continuum, anywhere from almost charming to grievously mean-spirited. Some people advocate for what they want with a smile on their face, but they have a second row of teeth behind that smile, like a shark ready to devour its prey. Others can be overtly bullish and intimidating, leaving a wake of injured people behind them. But no matter what method is used, the motive behind that method is what matters. Both types of people are motivated by their belief that they are right and the other person is wrong, or there would not be conflict.

Sometimes in a conflict, one person will say, "perception is reality," meaning, "since this is the way I perceive the situation, I am right." No. Truth is reality. And truth is comprised of the facts, not merely the feelings. The only way to truly resolve conflict is to embrace the truth. Jesus said, *"The truth will make you free"* (John 8:32 NASB).

Do you want to be free from the misery of conflict?

Embrace the truth.

Clear focus facilitates conflict resolution by embracing the truth. How? When we focus on Who (and who), our priorities are reset. We no longer think about ways to get what we want—we think about how to honor the Lord Jesus and how to meet the needs of those on whom His eyes are focused. This does not mean we ignore sins or offenses; neither does it mean that we simply allow others to do whatever they want to do.

The Bible gives clear instructions for how to approach these things. But our method of resolving the conflict is no longer flight or fight—it is love! Because we focus on Jesus, we see His love for the one with whom we are experiencing conflict. We see more clearly what He wants for that person—whatever is true, noble, right, pure, lovely, admirable, excellent, or praiseworthy (Phil. 4:8). Relational unity then becomes the higher goal of conflict resolution (Matt. 18:15-17; Eph. 4:2-3). We can then follow the biblical instructions on how to use a gentle approach to bring about restoration, especially whenever sin is involved (Gal. 6:1; 2 Tim. 2:24-26). Peace and mutual edification is the result of such conflict resolution (Matt. 6:9; Rom. 14:19; Heb. 12:14-15). *For harmony is as precious as the anointing oil that was poured over Aaron's head, that ran down his beard and onto the border of his robe* (Ps. 133:2 NLT).

The true motivation for conflict resolution is love. Jesus said, *"Love one another. As I have loved you, so you must love one another. By this everyone will know that you are my disciples, if you love one another"* (John 13:34-35). He prayed that we would have unity so the world would believe His Father sent Him (John 17:11, 21-23). Christian love is especially visible when believers can demonstrate it in the middle of conflict. Francis Schaeffer said,

> We are to love all true Christian brothers in a way that the world may observe. This means showing love to our brothers in the midst of our differences—great or small— loving our brothers when it costs us something, loving them even under times of tremendous emotional tension, loving them in a way the world can see. Love—and the unity it attests to—is the mark Christ gave Christians to wear before the world. Only with this mark may the world know that Christians are indeed Christians and that Jesus was sent by the Father.[48]

Restored relationships are worth the investment of time. With the help of the Holy Spirit, a commitment to listen carefully, an objective pursuit of factual truth (not only the emotions), and a gentle, anger-free approach will yield spiritual unity. James 3:17-18 says, *But the wisdom that comes from heaven is first of all pure; then peace-loving, considerate, submissive, full of mercy and good fruit, impartial and sincere. Peacemakers who sow in peace reap a harvest of righteousness.*

Years ago, a Christian friend and I were arguing vehemently about something. I honestly do not remember the source of our disagreement, but it became quite heated. One day we tried to discuss the cause of our conflict, but our anger with one another intensified, producing words that caused more damage in our relationship. Our conversation became louder and the tone of our voices became more and more aggressive. We were on the verge of damaging our friendship.

At that moment, another young man ran up to us and said, "I've been looking all over for both of you. I've been thinking about what you shared with me, and I've decided I want to become a Christian. What do I need to do?"

I am not exaggerating.

There we were—with red faces, angry spirits, and "righteous indignation" toward one another. But a who needed our attention in ministry for our Lord Jesus. My friend asked the young man if he could give us a moment. With that said, he extended his hand toward mine and humbly asked me to forgive him for the way he had been speaking to me. I was moved by his instant ability to repent, and I too asked for his forgiveness. Then together we prayed with our new brother in Christ, helping him receive the same kind of forgiveness we had just experienced from one another.

In the blink of an eye, our conflict was resolved because we focused on a who.

To this day, that brother remains a dear friend, and neither of us can remember what we argued about on that day.

# Clear Focus for God's Will Is Acquired through Peace

*I am leaving you with a gift—peace of mind and heart.*
*And the peace I give is a gift the world cannot give. So*
*don't be troubled or afraid.* John 14:27 (NLT)

For me, peace is more of an active word than a passive one. Sure, peace can be felt—a sense of serenity in place of fear or anxiety. But many times, a sense of peace confirms that we are traveling the right path, going in the right direction, or doing the right thing. If you have ever been lost, then you know exactly what I mean.

When my brother, David, and I were young, we went hiking on a nature trail at a local state park. The nature trails were clearly marked by blue or orange painted stripes on trees. On that particular day, we followed the orange trail. We did not know, however, that a logging company had been hired to mark trees in the forest to be harvested later that year. We assumed their orange flagging tape was the same as the orange painted stripes, so we followed what we thought was a new trail. After several hours of walking from one orange flag to another, we realized we were not returning to the parking lot where we had begun. We tried to find our way back, but everything looked different as evening approached.

When we realized we were lost, we panicked. My brother was three years younger, and I felt responsible for him. He was scared. I was scared. We had no peace. Then, by the providence of God, we stumbled upon a road. We walked down the road for quite some time before a car came along. Thankfully, the driver was a friendly man who offered to take us back to the parking lot. Our mother was more than relieved when we arrived. Once we were safely back where we were supposed to be, we had peace.

Peace is more than a feeling—it is a fact.

The feeling of peace comes from experiencing the fact that we are no longer lost from a lack of direction, lost from being embroiled in a conflict, or lost from being mired in a difficult set of circumstances. Peace can come from knowing this fact: even if we are lost, we can cast all our anxieties on the Lord because He cares for us (1 Peter 5:7). Peace also comes from experiencing the fact that we are doing what God wants us to do, and we are going where God wants us to go.

People often ask me, "How can I know for sure if God is leading me to do something?" The question itself emanates from some kind of dilemma or difficulty that has generated turmoil in the person's life. When we come to a crossroads in life or ministry, it is hard to know which road to take. Sometimes, both roads seem plausible. Other times, neither road looks desirable. So we hold a mental gymnastics event that leaves us anxious, fearful, or confused. In times like these, we simply want to know what God wants us to do. Until we do, our focus is unclear. We may feel like a wave in the sea, blown and tossed by the wind (James 1:6). We need God's wisdom, direction, and peace. Again, this kind of peace is more active than passive.

Some Christians follow what they call an open-or-closed-door approach to discovering the will of God: if they walk by faith toward something, God will close the door if it is not what He wants. Certainly, that is possible. But is it also possible that other people or the devil could close the door? We also could close it by simply convincing ourselves of what we want or do not want. Of course, God could intervene if He chose to do so, but this approach to understanding God's will is based purely on circumstances. If the circumstances line up, it must be God's will.

Other believers look for a sign from heaven to know whether something is God's will. This is similar to the first approach—purely based on circumstances—but in this case, only God controls the circumstances. The rationale for this approach may be based on Gideon's fleece, but note that God had already told Gideon what to do before he put out the fleece (Judg. 6:14). Gideon was afraid and he needed reassurance. (Remember, the fleece in his case sent him into battle—a battle for which God asked him to reduce his army to only 300 men!)

God can and does control circumstances in our lives.

But that is not the only way He leads us.

Sometimes the fleece approach is filled with "miraculous" provisions from God—everything from a divinely appointed parking space at the mall to getting the dream job. But on closer inspection, the "will of God" always seems to be aligned with our comfort or convenience. That seems so different from the prayer Jesus prayed in the Garden of Gethsemane, while He sweat drops of blood: *"Father, if you are willing, take this cup from me; yet not my will, but yours be done"* (Luke 22:42). And during this time of prayer with His Father, Jesus acquired the clear focus He needed to face the cross.

To acquire clear focus and to know what God wants us to do, we have to understand how His peace works in our lives to confirm His will. After all, the Kingdom of God is *righteousness, peace and joy in the Holy Spirit* (Rom. 14:17). Jesus taught us to pray for His kingdom to come and His will to be done on earth as it is in heaven (Matt. 6:10). Most of the time, we struggle to find the will of God because our focus is on a what instead of a who. We make mental (or physical) lists of pros and cons, trying to compute the advantages or disadvantages of a particular decision or direction. Then, after we have exhausted ourselves mentally and emotionally by trying to *lean on our own understanding*, we come back to the simple truth that we need to *trust in the LORD with all [our] heart* and allow Him *to make [our] paths straight* (Prov. 3:5-6 NASB, emphasis mine). We should have sought God's kingdom first, along with His righteousness, realizing that He will take care of all the whats for us (Matt. 6:33).

Paul reminds us to *let the peace of Christ rule in [our] hearts* (Col. 3:15). The word *rule* in this verse describes an umpire settling a matter of dispute. In other words, it is necesary to let the peace of Christ be the *decider* of all things within our hearts.[49] When we give the Lord our bodies as a living sacrifice (the way Jesus did on our behalf), and when we allow Him to transform us by the renewing of our minds with His truth, we can know His good, pleasing, and perfect will (Rom. 12:1-2).

This is one way we can recognize something is God's will: it will equip us to think more highly of others and serve them selflessly (Rom. 12:3; Phil. 2:3-4).

The peace of God then comes as a confirmation. And peace is often combined with another fruit of the Spirit—joy in knowing God is pleased with our decision to trust His will for us. God will keep us in perfect peace as our mind is focused on Him, trusting fully in His sovereign plan (Isa. 26:3).

Jesus is called the Prince of Peace (Isa. 9:6). How was peace possible for the disciples in the storm, the demon-possessed man, the woman with the issue of blood, and Jairus's family on that incredible day? In all four cases, they ran to Jesus, and He generated the peace they needed so they could clearly focus. The first step toward obtaining a clear focus is running to Jesus—focusing on Who. Once He speaks, *"Peace, be still,"* we can better understand what He wants us to do (Mark 4:39 NKJV). And what a remarkable privilege it is, when He uses us to speak peace into the lives of the special whos He has placed in our lives.

# CHAPTER 8

# Focus in Action

*I will show you my faith by what I do.* James 2:18 (NCV)

As Dutch eyeglass maker Hans Lippershey watched some children playing with two lenses in his shop, he came up with the idea for the telescope in 1608 and obtained its first patent. One year later, Galileo improved the design and used it to see craters on the moon, view the Milky Way, and learn that Jupiter had its own moons.[50] In 1637, René Descartes said, "By taking our sense of sight far beyond the realm of our forebearers' imagination, these wonderful instruments, the telescopes, open the way to a deeper and more perfect understanding of nature."[51]

Over the last 400 years, man's quest to build larger and more powerful telescopes has been nearly insatiable. We have even launched telescopes into outer space, including the Hubble Space Telescope initiated in 1990. The newest and most ambitious telescope is currently being constructed in Hawaii, and it is scheduled to be fully operational in 2022. Thirty Meter Telescope is aptly named for its 30-meter mirror (made from 492 smaller mirrors designed to fit flawlessly together to form one enormous mirror). It will collect 144 times more light than the Hubble Space Telescope, making it possible to look deep into the cosmos to see distant galaxies.[52]

Why do we want to build bigger telescopes? To see what we cannot see with our naked eye (or with previous magnifiers). If there is something to see "out there," we desperately want to see it. We want to know whatever (whoever) there is to know, so we take action. We believe, so we act. We spend untold fortunes and entire lifetimes to build stronger, more powerful telescopes, hoping they will reveal the secrets and origins of the universe. Of course, as Christians, we believe God created the heavens and the earth. Everything we see through the lens of a telescope serves to further encourage our worship and adoration of the Maker of heaven and earth. Isaiah 40:26 says,

> *Lift up your eyes and look to the heavens:*
> *Who created all these? He who brings out the starry host one*
> *by one and calls forth each of them by name. Because of his*
> *great power and mighty strength, not one of them is missing.*

We may very well have it backwards. While we seek to expand our view deeper into the cosmos, God actually has His "telescope" pointed at us. *God looks down from heaven on the children of man to see if there are any who understand, who seek after God* (Ps. 53:2 ESV). Unfortunately, the psalmist goes on to say that God does not find anyone seeking after Him—not even one.

Paul echoes this truth in Romans 3:11, then reveals how God took action. He sent Jesus to serve as a sacrifice of atonement through the shedding of His blood to make us righteous, redeeming us as His own (Rom. 3:24-25). God also sends His ambassadors of *the message of reconciliation* to make it possible for us to be restored in our relationship with our Creator (2 Cor. 5:19-20). As Christian school educators, we have the incredible opportunity to participate with God as His agents of action toward those in His focus. This means our focus on whos needs to be active.

## Magnify the Potential

*I am certain that God, who began the good work within you, will continue his work until it is finally finished on the day when Christ Jesus returns.* Philippians 1:6 (NLT)

I must have been in elementary school when I first looked through a microscope at the slide of an amoeba. It left a lasting impression. When I looked through the lens, I did not see anything but a fuzzy blur. The girl in line before me wore glasses, so when she looked through the lens, she must have adjusted the focusing knob. I had not listened closely to the teacher's instructions, so I did not know I could turn the focusing knob and see what everyone else was excitedly describing: the nucleus, the membrane, the endoplasm. I was so disappointed. Thankfully, the teacher then showed me how to adjust the focusing knob, and with that magnified focus, I could explore a whole new world.

In a similar way, a whole new world of ministry can be opened before us once we adjust our focus away from the blurry distractions of excessive whats toward a clear focus of Who (and who). Notice Paul's excitement when he focused his attention on the whos in Ephesus:

*I pray that from his glorious, unlimited resources he will empower you with inner strength through his Spirit. Then Christ will make his home in your hearts as you trust in him. Your roots will grow down into God's love and keep you strong. And may you have the power to understand, as all God's people should, how wide, how long, how high, and how deep his love is. May you experience the love of Christ, though it is too great to understand fully. Then you will be made complete with all the fullness of life and power that comes from God. Now all glory to God, who is able, through his mighty power at work within us, to accomplish infinitely more than we might ask or think. Glory to him in the church and in Christ Jesus through all generations forever and ever! Amen.* (Eph. 3:16-20 NLT)

Wow! Paul looked at the believers in Ephesus through a spiritual magnifying glass, which allowed him to see all their potential in Christ Jesus. He could see the power and strength they were receiving from the Holy Spirit. He could see their roots growing deep into the love of God, and he knew that love would make them complete and fulfilled. But beyond that, Paul could see with eyes of faith how God was able, through His mighty power at work in them, to accomplish *infinitely more than we might ask or think* (Eph 3:20).

Through eyes of faith, we can magnify the potential we see in others. We can look past what we see now and envision all they could become—really more than we can ask or imagine when God's mighty power is at work in them.

For example, Peter used eyes of faith to see the man at the temple gate called Beautiful. Surely, he and the other disciples had seen this man many times as they had entered the temple—he had been there since birth. On previous trips, maybe Peter had ignored him along with the other beggars. Or perhaps he had given him a coin or two in the past. But this time was different. Now Peter had the power of the Holy Spirit surging through him, helping him to magnify his focus on a who, which then propelled him to a higher level of action. *And fixing his eyes on him, with John, Peter said, "Look at us"* (Acts 3:4 NKJV).

Do not miss Peter's focus.

He saw the potential in this man to be *walking and jumping, and praising God* in the temple courts instead of being carried to the gate each day to beg for money (Acts 3:8). With this kind of faith-filled focus, Peter said to the man, *"Silver or gold I do not have, but what I do have I give you. In the name of Jesus Christ of Nazareth, walk"* (Acts 4:6). And he did!

One day a teacher came to talk with me about a difficult student in her classroom. He was rambunctiously disobedient and constantly distracting others; therefore, he required more and more of her attention. Ironically, he was one of her best students academically, and she believed he had leadership potential. He was always sorry for his actions whenever she and his parents confronted him, but his poor behavior in class was growing worse, and she wondered if he could change. She had reached her wits' end with him and wanted me to intervene.

I advised her to try a different approach for a week or two to see if it would help. I said, "Imagine that you are very old and lying on your deathbed. Someone called for your pastor to come read Psalm 23 to you and to pray with you before taking your last breath. When he arrives, you look up and see your student's face. He is now your pastor, shepherding you through the final transition to your heavenly home." I was encouraging her to view her student through eyes of faith, envisioning all he could be and magnifying the potential he had with God's mighty power working in his life.

Things changed that day for both the teacher and the student.

Sure, it was a process, but she had learned to see his potential, and it made her efforts worth the investment.

It is easy to forget the impact we can make if we see our students through eyes of faith. On the acknowledgements page of this book, I recognized my fifth grade teacher, Miss Ramsey. I do not remember many details about elementary school, but I will never forget one specific day in her class. On that day, she read to the entire class a short story I had written, and then she pinned it on the bulletin board, where the large red A printed at the top of my paper could be seen easily. In addition, when other teachers visited our room, Miss Ramsey showed them my short story and said, "I'm looking forward to reading the books Stephen writes when he becomes an author." I have held that statement in my heart, and it has inspired me to write. Miss Ramsey saw the potential in me and spoke it by faith. As you read this book, you are also experiencing the outcome of her faith.

As Christian school educators, we should attempt to see our students through eyes of faith, seeing the evidence of what God says they can be—not necessarily what our physical eyes see at any given moment.

We may have to close our eyes so we can see that which is invisible.

We may need to close our ears so we can hear what God is saying about our students. One of them may be the next Daniel, Ruth, Paul, or Billy Graham.

God has placed our students in Christian schools to prepare and equip them as His masterpieces—*created in Christ Jesus to do good works which God prepared in advance for [them] to do* (Eph. 2:10). We can be certain that God will complete the work He has begun in the lives of our students

(Phil. 1:6). So we should keep our eyes fixed on the author and finisher of our faith. We must focus on that which is eternal—invisible—not allowing what is visible to weaken our faith. Then like Abraham, who believed God could raise the dead and therefore received Isaac back from the dead, we should ensure our actions match our faith-filled focus on the whos in our lives (Heb. 11:18-19).

# Reach Out to the Unreachable

*He reached down from heaven and rescued me; he*
*drew me out of deep waters.* Psalm 18:16 (NLT)

My favorite detail about the day Jesus and His disciples went over to the other side of the Sea of Galilee to rescue the demon-possessed man is that he was "unreachable." Based on the scriptural accounts, the only thing people had tried to do with this man was to restrain him—and even that was unsuccessful. Maybe at some point someone had tried to reach out to him—a family member, a friend, or possibly a compassionate stranger. But the man's life was so terrible—as many as 6,000 demons lived in him— that he seemed truly unreachable, at least from a human perspective. Max Lucado describes the man this way:

> Wiry, clumpy hair. A beard to the chest, ribboned with blood. Furtive eyes, darting in all directions, refusing to fix. Naked. No sandals to protect feet from the rocks of the ground or clothing to protect skin from the rocks in his hand. He beats himself with stones. Bruises blotch his skin like ink stains. Open sores and gashes attract flies. His home is a limestone mausoleum, a graveyard of Galilean shoreline caves cut out of the cliffs. Apparently he feels more secure among the dead than the living.[53]

But then he met Jesus!

I have changed the title in my Bible from "The Demon-possessed Man" to "The First Missionary to the Gentiles." Why? A year and a half later, when Jesus and His disciples returned to that region, they were met by more than 4,000 people on the shore, who had brought their sick friends and relatives to Jesus (Mark 7:31-8:9; Matt. 15:29-38). From where did these people come? They came from the ten cities of the Decapolis where this first missionary told others how much Jesus had done for him. And because of the strong link these ten cities had with Rome, some of these believers may have carried the good news of Jesus Christ there as well. About fifty years later, when the apostle Paul wrote his letter to the church at Rome, a large

Gentile Christian population already existed in Rome.[54] Some of these Gentile believers may have come from the Decapolis as well as from other regions where the gospel had been preached since it was said that "all roads led to Rome."[55] And from Rome, the gospel spread to the entire world.

Is it possible that this formerly demon-possessed man could be the missionary who first shared the gospel with Gentiles who went on to share it with my ancestors in Europe?

Look what can happen when Jesus focuses on an unreachable individual—a desperate who.

When my son, Christopher, was serving as a short-term missionary in South Africa, he wrote this blogpost:

> I remember one day when I was serving at the Dwaleni Feeding Program so vividly. It was just one of those days where you struggle to get out of bed and you feel ineffective the whole day long. My fingernails were black from scrubbing a pot with burned beans on the bottom. The ladies in the kitchen were laughing at me because I wasn't doing it fast enough—since I was a male. I joked with another volunteer that only God would have made me semi-happy to wash dishes in this place. I can't even stand to load the dishwasher at home; the dried-on food makes me sick. I wondered what small things Jesus might have done in His ministry. John 21 tells us that if everything that Jesus did were written down, the whole world couldn't hold the amount of books it would take to tell the stories. I quoted Mother Teresa: "We can do no great things, only small things with great love." Just then I felt a hand tug at mine. I looked down and saw the most beautiful face I think I've ever seen. He was no more than five years old. His brown eyes seemed to illuminate his little black face. He wrapped his tiny palm around mine and just stared into my eyes. It seemed like hours in that moment. It was all I could do to fight back the tears of knowing that I was right where I was supposed to be. My dad often tells me, the impact that you will make in life may not be something

you will even know you did. It may be something small, something trivial in your mind that will change the world. It might be holding someone's hand, and in that moment— even if only for that moment—they know they are loved.[79]

*This is what real love is: It is not our love for God; it is God's love for us. He sent his Son to die in our place to take away our sins* (1 John 4:10 NCV). Jesus knew we were desperate, drowning in our sin. *While we were still sinners, Christ died for us* (Rom. 5:8). As we fix our focus on Jesus and see His great love for desperate sinners, He will produce that same kind of love in us for desperate whos. We will become more aware of *the least of these* in our midst (Matt. 25:40). With the love of Christ, we will look for opportunities to reach out to those who are desperate.

I am always grateful whenever I see people sacrificially reaching out, often as missionaries, (foreign and domestic), to extend Jesus' love to those who would not otherwise experience it. The first thing we usually notice about people who have a life-changing encounter with Jesus is that they immediately reach out to others to share their newfound joy and hope. Their focus on Who generates an immediate focus on whos. That is what happened to the demon-possessed man (Mark 5:20), the woman Jesus met at the well (John 4:29, 39), and countless others to whom He ministered.

Desperate people surround us. We are all desperate for Jesus more than we realize. Stop for a moment and consider where you would be without Him. Are you glad that He focused His attention on you to rescue you from your desperation?

Mother Teresa, famous for her commitment to whos, (the most desperate souls in India) said,

> Stay where you are. Find your own Calcutta. Find the sick, the suffering and the lonely right there where you are—in your own homes and in your own families, in your workplaces and in your schools.... You can find Calcutta all over the world, if you have the eyes to see. Everywhere, wherever you go, you find people who are unwanted, unloved, uncared for, just rejected by society— completely forgotten, completely left alone.[56]

# Encourage the Discouraged and Disqualified

*Most of the important things in the world have been accomplished by people who have kept on trying when there seemed to be no hope at all.* Dale Carnegie[57]

A few years ago, I took a group of high school boys rappelling in the North Carolina mountains. I was a rappelling instructor in the USMC and had rappelled hundreds of times in many different situations, so I probably selected a site that was a bit too aggressive for first-timers. (Think Pride Rock in *The Lion King*.) After tying off the rope, I asked for a volunteer to go first—a backward step off a 150-foot precipice. One brave young man stepped forward. I hooked in his snap link and told him to start leaning back over the edge and trust the rope. He was trying to be strong, but as he looked over his shoulder, his knees shook and buckled beneath him. As he trembled, I reassured him to trust the rope while I placed both of my hands around the rope in front of him. As he was leaning backward over the precipice at a 90-degree angle, I reminded him, "Don't look down. Trust the rope—it will hold you."

He pleaded with me, "Don't let go."

I said, "I know you can trust this rope because I have trusted it many times with my own life." Then I suddenly lifted both my hands in the air, revealing to him that I had not been holding the rope at all. The rope had been holding him the entire time.

His eyes widened and almost instantly his courage returned. He descended with whoops of triumph!

His nervous friends were then encouraged and ready to do it too.

Encouragement is like that. It gives courage to others—especially to those who may have become discouraged. Discouragement is the opposite of encouragement. The Hebrew word for *discouraged* in Joshua 1:9 can also be translated *dismayed*. It means to become faint-hearted or to have one's confidence shattered.[58] This occurs when the circumstances of life overwhelm us and create such fear that our knees buckle. Jesus said, "*The thief comes only to steal and kill and destroy*"—the result of which is discouragement—"*I came that they may have life and have it abundantly*" (John 10:10 ESV). He wants to restore our confidence and our courage by connecting us to His life (the True Rope) that will hold us up and never disappoint us. Our job as encouragers is to convey that message to others who need it most. Aubrey Johnson says,

> Encouragers are people who are unusually effective in relating to others in a positive way. They are pleasant to be around because of their optimism and enthusiasm about life. They radiate a quiet self-confidence, which enables them to focus on others rather than demanding constant attention to fulfill their emotional needs.[59]

Encouragement requires a time investment, which may be the reason it is such a rare commodity in our relationships. It takes intentionality to recognize those who may be discouraged, compassion to seek them out, and careful listening to understand their need and meet it. In *Encouraging the Heart*, Kouzes and Posner said,

> Eyes-and-heart listening can't be from a distance…. Our constituents want to know who we are, how we feel, and whether we really care. They want to see us in living color. Since proximity is the best predictor of whether two people will talk to one another, you have to get close to people if you're going to communicate…. We have to go to them.[60]

Encouragers are those who are ready to help restore the courage of others because they are already fully connected to and relying completely on the True Rope—Jesus Christ. They are completely focused on Who. In Colossians 2:1-2, Paul wrote,

> *I want you to know how hard I am contending for you and for those at Laodicea, and for all who have not met me personally. My goal is that they may be encouraged in heart and united in love, so that they may have the full riches of complete understanding, in order that they may know the mystery of God, namely, Christ.*

When we come alongside someone who has become discouraged, we are actually enabling that person to overcome a difficult circumstance with confidence and gallantry. We encourage them to trust in the Lord, and we provide the supportive strength they need. Paul described this as being *united in love*. Through God's love, we become intertwined and inseparable from other believers, which combines our strength. This is similar to the rappelling rope. It is comprised of many strands of nylon string that have been woven together to provide strength that far exceeds what is needed to support the weight. God desires that we actively build up one another by using encouraging words of affirmation as often as possible. We give joy and energy to others by investing in their lives through positive and supportive words of encouragement, which may sound like this:

> Be strong. Never give up. I believe in you.
> Be bold and courageous. Do not be afraid.
> The LORD your God is with you. I am with you!

One common source of discouragement is failure. Most of us have experienced failure at some point in our Christian lives and ministries, which may cause us to either give up or want to give up. In those times, we need someone to come alongside us to believe in us, encourage us, and strengthen us to continue in the faith.

During the early growth of the New Testament church, a young man named John Mark, originally from Cyprus, was eager to be a part of Paul's exciting evangelistic ministry. Along with his cousin, Joseph, (also from Cyprus), he signed up to go with Paul on his first missionary journey. After only a few stops on the trip, for some reason, John Mark became discouraged. Maybe he was homesick. Maybe he had not anticipated the difficulty of missionary work—especially the opposition they encountered. Maybe he became disillusioned with some aspect of the ministry—perhaps there were not enough whats to meet his expectation. We do not know why, but for whatever reason, he abandoned the mission and returned home a failed missionary. That decision disqualified him for future service in Paul's mind. Later, when John Mark's cousin, Joseph, advocated that he be given another opportunity to serve on the next missionary journey,

Paul sharply disagreed. But Joseph did not give up on John Mark. In fact, he took John Mark with him to do some missionary work in Cyprus.

Joseph was known by another name—a nickname given to him by the apostles—Barnabas, which means "son of encouragement" (Acts 4:36). Can you imagine someone being so consistently encouraging that he was given that nickname? Barnabas is the name Luke used for Joseph in the rest of his narrative in the Book of Acts. Barnabas had encouraged the apostles to receive Saul after his conversion to Christianity (Acts 9:27). He also encouraged the growth of Christianity in the church at Antioch, one of the largest cities in the Roman Empire (Acts 11:23-24). And Barnabas advocated for his cousin, John Mark, to have another chance in ministry after he had disqualified himself. I am so glad he did. In later years, John Mark served effectively with both Peter and Paul in their ministries (Col. 4:10; 2 Tim. 4:11; 1 Peter 5:13).

He also wrote a well-known book.

Perhaps you have read it: the Gospel of Mark.

Each of us has needed or will need encouragement from someone like Barnabas. We all become discouraged at some point along the way. Many of us have even disqualified ourselves from Christian service. But God, who is rich in mercy, will send someone into our lives to supply the courage we need to continue on in our faith. Bill Hybels reminds us:

> [The body of Christ serves as] a living, breathing, pulsating organism that is evolving in real-time based on the thousand ways we choose to care for each other, listen to each other, hold each other up when the rug has just been yanked out from beneath our feet.[61]

Who is your John Mark?

# Restore the *Imago Dei*

*He leads me beside the still waters. He restores*
*my soul.* Psalm 23:2-3 (NKJV)

A famous statue of Adam, by fifteenth-century Venetian sculptor Tullio Lombardo, is on prominent display in Gallery 534 at the Metropolitan Museum of Art in New York City. On October 6, 2002, the wooden pedestal holding the six-foot-three, 770-pound marble sculpture buckled under the statue's weight. It collapsed and fell to the floor. Adam smashed into hundreds of pieces; his head separated from his body. A team of scientists and engineers spent twelve years restoring the 500-year-old sculpture.

Museum Director, Mr. de Montebello, said he wanted Adam returned to a condition so perfect that only Lombardo could tell anything had happened. "The aesthetic of Tullio is largely dependent on the high finish of the piece," he said. "To leave it in a broken state would have been to choose its accident as its defining historical moment."

The latest technology was used to put Adam back together, including laser-mapping, CT scanning, and the use of innovative fiberglass pins for increased weight-bearing and safety. The final piece was the sculpture's head, which was reattached on April 1, 2013. After all the holes from the pulverized marble had been filled and colored to match the original stone, Adam was cleaned, polished, and placed on display with the title: After the Fall: The Conservation of Tullio Lombardo's *Adam*.[62]

One of the greatest privileges we have as servants of God, invited to join Him in His eternal work, is to be His instruments of restoration with the whos He has placed in our lives. God is restoring believers to the *Imago Dei*, (His image and His likeness) through the sanctifying power of His word and His Spirit. We are putting on *the new self, which is being renewed in knowledge in the image of its Creator* (Col. 3:10). As Christian school educators, we are the skilled artisans God uses to craft and shape His handiwork—our students—for the work He has prepared for them to do in His eternal kingdom (Eph. 2:10). Before we can do this effectively, we must fully realize that each of us is someone God has restored.

God created us to be His image bearers (Gen. 1:27; James 3:9). We were designed to look and act like Him—reflect His glory. But through the sinful fall of Adam and Eve, and the entire human race as a result (Rom. 5:12), that image has been marred. The museum director's quote is profound: "To leave [the statue] in a broken state would have been to choose its accident as its defining historical moment." Praise God for His *abundant provision of grace and of the gift of righteousness* through our Lord Jesus Christ (Rom. 5:17). He did not leave us in our broken state; He made provision for us to be fully restored to His image and likeness.

When I realize that we, as Christian school educators, are privileged to be like those museum conservators and engineers in the lives of our students, under the masterful direction of the Holy Spirit—reassembling, restoring, cleaning, and polishing them to look like their original design— it is both overwhelming and rewarding. I am humbled that God would allow me to be included in His team of experts to restore such a valuable work of art, far more valuable than a Renaissance statue.

Joy McCullough provides a number of important considerations for Christian educators to remember when it comes to being restored to the *Imago Dei*:

- Unity – our nature is to mirror God as a unity (body, soul, spirit). God has created us with a nature in which our body, soul, and spirit are meant to work together in unity.
- Rationality – we are able to think and understand, and we desire a logical and orderly environment to live in. Because we reflect God, we seek structure, organization, and patterns to make sense of created reality.
- Interactivity – we are always in relationship with God, with others, and with creation. God is triune, and He lives in relationship as the Father, Son, and Holy Spirit.
- Moral Awareness – we can determine right from wrong, good from evil. He created us with an inborn moral compass that is set to His standard.
- Creativity – we can copy an original, can create a new product, and can appreciate the beauty of God's creation. As image bearers of God, we are created to be creative.[63]

God is restoring us to His original design. Our role as Christian educators is to participate with Him in that process, helping our students become more and more like Him *as we are changed into His glorious image* (2 Cor. 3:18 NLT). God designed us to be holy—capable of discerning and knowing absolute truth. He made us to be like Him—loving, merciful, faithful, and powerful to serve on His behalf in His kingdom. Being restored is essential for our usefulness. And it takes someone focused on the whos, not the whats, to initiate the process.

Consider how Paul focused on restoration in his ministry to a runaway slave from Colessae named Onesimus. If caught, under Roman law, Onesimus could face possible torture or death by crucifixion. But somehow, in his running, the fugitive ran into Paul, who was imprisoned in Rome. Onesimus also ran into the gospel of Jesus Christ, and after he became a believer, he was "useful" to Paul—a pun on his name, Onesimus. And Paul accepted God's assignment to restore the formerly desperate who (Philem. 1-25).

At first glance, Onesimus may seem to lack the potential for restoration. If he stayed in Rome, he would remain a criminal on the run. If he returned to his master, Philemon, in Colessae, he would face extreme punishment and possible death. Paul stepped into Onesimus's story and became an intercessor on his behalf. He advocated for him to be restored—not as a slave, but as a brother in Christ. Can you hear the chain around Paul's wrist clinking (he was shackled to a Roman soldier in prison) as he wrote a letter with his own hand begging Philemon to restore Onesimus?

*I, Paul, an old man now and also a prisoner for Christ Jesus, am pleading with you for my child Onesimus, who became my child while I was in prison. In the past he was useless to you, but now he has become useful for both you and me. I am sending him back to you, and with him I am sending my own heart. I wanted to keep him with me so that in your place he might help me while I am in prison for the Good News. But I did not want to do anything without asking you first so that any good you do for me will be because you want to do it, not because I forced you. Maybe Onesimus was separated from you for a short time so you could have him back forever—no longer as a slave, but better than a slave, as a loved brother. I love him very much, but you will love him even more, both as a person and as a believer in the Lord.*

*So if you consider me your partner, welcome Onesimus as you would welcome me. If he has done anything wrong to you or if he owes you anything, charge that to me. I, Paul, am writing this with my own hand. I will pay it back, and I will say nothing about what you owe me for your own life. So, my brother, I ask that you do this for me in the Lord: Refresh my heart in Christ. I write this letter, knowing that you will do what I ask you and even more.* (Philem. 1: 9-21 NCV)

We do not know how Philemon responded to Paul's letter, but since he was a leader in the Colossian church, I can only hope that he granted Paul's request. Can you see Onesimus humbly standing before the church congregation at Colessae alongside Tychicus, Paul's faithful letter carrier, who had accompanied the runaway slave on the trip from Rome? Everyone in the church knew Onesimus was a wanted criminal, but he also had become a vivid picture of grace—a portrait of restoration. Paul believed in him, saw him as useful in the ministry, and even offered to repay his debt to Philemon.

Is there an Onesimus in your life?

Has God asked you to focus on a broken student who needs to be restored?

# Take Action in His Strength

*Be strong in the Lord and in the strength of
his might.* Ephesians 6:10 (ESV)

"Are those Oreo cookies? I love Oreos," boomed a deep voice behind me.

I glanced over my shoulder to see one of the largest men I had ever seen standing behind me. He held out his enormous hand, and I handed him my newly opened package of Oreos. I have never seen anyone eat an entire pack of cookies in two or three bites, but after he finished, he patted me on the back and walked away, leaving me holding the empty wrapper.

As it turned out, that was one of the best investments I ever made.

Private Chase (about six feet four and 250 pounds of muscle) was in my infantry training school company—one of two hundred men. Only four of us ended up in the same unit on the other side of the world after training, and Chase was one of them. Shortly after I arrived on the base, I was cornered by three other Marines—part of a hazing initiation for newbies. Being of average size, I was certainly no match for three of them. At that moment, Chase stepped around the corner and stood behind me. He said, "Reel, are you about to fight? I love to fight." My three would-be aggressors quickly made excuses and dismissed themselves. For the next four years, Chase was my guardian angel and close friend. His strength became a source of strength for me—and we consumed many Oreo cookies together. Leading this giant man to a saving knowledge of Jesus Christ was one of my greatest joys.

Taking action in our ministry as Christian school educators requires major strength—and it cannot come only from us. I have met too many teachers, support staff, and leaders in Christian schools who say they have reached the end of their proverbial rope and they are holding on for dear life. They are merely surviving. But God wants much more than that for those who serve in His kingdom. He wants us to be strong, courageous, unafraid, and undiscouraged, for the Lord our God is with us wherever we go (Josh. 1:9). His presence can exhilarate us, and His strength can invigorate us.

We must not underestimate the strength God gives us to serve on His behalf. He knows we are made out of clay; we are weak and fragile without His provision of power. *But we have this treasure in jars of clay to show that this all-surpassing power is from God and not from us* (2 Cor. 4:7). This power is *the same as the mighty strength he exerted when he raised Christ from the dead and seated him at his right hand in the heavenly realms* (Eph. 1:19-20).

Why do we try to serve in our own strength when we have the resurrection power of Christ available for our ministry? The Lord told Paul, *"When you are weak, my power is made perfect in you"* (2 Cor. 12:9 NCV). That is the reason Paul could write, *I delight in weaknesses, in insults, in hardships, in persecutions, in difficulties. For when I am weak, then I am strong* (2 Cor. 12:10).

Earlier we discussed the importance of being yoked with Christ, relying on His strength so our burden remains light (Matt. 11:30). We should honestly assess whether we are serving in His strength or our own. Even if we are able to focus on whos, we will be ineffective in taking action if we rely on our own strength—a serious issue for many in the ministry of Christian education.

Paul said his desire was to *present everyone fully mature in Christ* (Col. 1:28). This is our goal as well. Pay close attention to what he said next: *To do this, I work and struggle,* using Christ's great strength *that works so powerfully in me* (Col. 1:29 NCV, emphasis mine). Paul worked and struggled, but he did not do that with his own strength. He did it with the strength of Jesus Christ working powerfully in him. Jesus said, *"Apart from me, you can do nothing"* (John 15:5).

Max Lucado says, "Much of life is spent rowing. Getting out of bed. Fixing lunches. Turning in assignments. Changing diapers. Paying bills. Routine. Regular. More struggle than strut. More wrestling than resting."[64] Rowing is hard work especially in difficult seas. Mark's description was *straining at the oars* (Mark 6:48). How many times do we feel like our ministry in Christian school education is rowing—straining at the oars? We want desperately to accomplish the work we have been called to do, but our strength is gone and we feel weak. In those situations, we need to focus on Who. Psalm 105:4 says, *Look to the LORD and His strength; seek His face always.* Sure, much of life and ministry is rowing, but it is worth the effort if Jesus is in the boat. It is worth the effort if lives are changed for eternity.

You may say, "All of this sounds great. I need God's strength to help me do what He has called me to do. But I am so weak at this point, I don't even have enough strength to look to the Lord to seek His face." That is an honest assessment of how many who serve in Christian ministry feel at times. They are spent. Exhausted. Ready to give up.

But I have good news for you.

God has provided us with some specialized help for times like this. Paul writes,

> *Likewise the Spirit helps us in our weakness. For we do not know what to pray for as we ought, but the Spirit himself intercedes for us with groanings too deep for words.* (Rom. 8:26 ESV)

The Greek word Paul used for *weakness* in this verse is *asthéneia*, which literally means to be *without strength*—translated strengthlessness, impotence, physical weakness, or feeble.[65] Paul used this same word to define his own weakness in 2 Corinthians 12:10. When people say they do not have the strength to pray, God completely understands, so He sends the Holy Spirit to help us.

Paul also used a unique word for *help* in this verse to describe the kind of help the Holy Spirit gives us when we are without strength. The Greek word is *synantilambano* [*syn* - together with; *anti* - face to face; *lambano* - to take hold of].[66] In effect, Paul is saying that when we are weak, the Holy Spirit comes alongside us, stands face to face with us, takes hold of us in our "strengthlessness," and intercedes in prayer for us. This is the source of the power that enables us to serve in the strength of Christ. No wonder Paul could go on to say, *We know that in all things God works for the good of those who love him, who have been called according to his purpose* (Rom. 8:28). That is the reason Paul gladly delighted in his weaknesses—so Christ's power would rest on him. He knew that in weakness, he could truly exhibit God's strength.

Remember, God chooses the *weak things of this world to shame the strong* (1 Cor. 1:27). Perhaps He allows us to become weak at certain times so we can serve Him more effectively—in His power instead of our own. Jesus was *crucified in weakness, yet he lives by God's power. Likewise, we are weak in him, yet by God's power we will live with him in our dealing with you* (2 Cor. 13:4). By remaining in God's presence, we find our strength to serve as He comes alongside us to give us His power and protection.

Joshua relied on the presence and power of the Lord when he led Israel into the Promised Land. He knew God would honor His promise to be with him wherever he needed to go because he had developed a lifestyle of staying in the presence of the Lord (Josh. 1:9). Joshua had several experiences with his mentor, Moses, which taught him to value God's presence over everything else. Joshua was in the presence of the Lord with Moses on Mt. Sinai when he received the Ten Commandments (Ex. 24:13-14). He was in the presence of the Lord with Moses in the Tent of Meeting where Moses met with the Lord *face to face, as a man speaks to his friend* (Ex. 33:11 ESV). Joshua remained there in God's presence after Moses left (Ex. 33:10-12). When Joshua was named Moses' successor, he was described as a man *in whom is [God's] Spirit* (Num. 27:18 NKJV). Joshua was also one of the twelve spies sent into Canaan, and he led the battle in the defeat of the Amalakites when Aaron and Hur held up Moses' hands (Num. 13-14; Ex. 17:8-14). Joshua knew what it meant to rely on the presence and power of the Lord.

In the same way, we must value God's presence and power in our life and ministry so we can take action in His strength. Isaiah 41:10 says,

> *So do not fear, for I am with you; do not be dismayed, for I am your God. I will strengthen you and help you; I will uphold you with my righteous right hand.*

If you read this chapter and admittedly feel weak in your own walk with the Lord or in your ministry, please read it again. Pause at each Scripture reference and meditate on God's Word, allowing it to build (or rebuild) your faith. Spend time in the presence of the Lord, and allow the Holy Spirit to strengthen you, taking hold of your weakness and giving you His power. Servants need strength to serve. We cannot effectively focus on the whos until we have intently focused on Who, receiving His great strength, which will work powerfully in and through us.

# Battle from an Angel's Perspective

> *Then I looked and heard the voice of many angels,*
> *numbering thousands upon thousands, and ten thousand*
> *times ten thousand. They encircled the throne and the*
> *living creatures and the elders. In a loud voice they*
> *were saying: "Worthy is the Lamb, who was slain, to*
> *receive power and wealth and wisdom and strength and*
> *honor and glory and praise!"* Revelation 5:11-12

Have you ever wondered what we might look like from an angel's point of view? The spiritual realm around us is invisible to our human eyes, but it is real. A major spiritual battle is being fought all around us between the angels of God and *the spiritual forces of evil in the heavenly realms* (Eph. 6:12), and we are the main actors on the stage of the Kingdom of God. Remember when an enemy army had surrounded Elisha and his servant, and Elisha asked God to open his servant's eyes to see the angelic forces that protected them?

> *"Don't be afraid," the prophet answered. "Those who are*
> *with us are more than those who are with them." And Elisha*
> *prayed, "Open his eyes, LORD, so that he may see." Then*
> *the LORD opened the servant's eyes, and he looked and saw*
> *the hills full of horses and chariots of fire all around Elisha.*
> (2 Kings 6:16-17)

That must have been a remarkable sight! Daniel also gives a vivid description of an angel:

> *I looked up and there before me was a man dressed in linen,*
> *with a belt of fine gold from Uphaz around his waist. His*
> *body was like topaz, his face like lightning, his eyes like*
> *flaming torches, his arms and legs like the gleam of burnished*
> *bronze, and his voice like the sound of a multitude.* (Dan.
> 10:5-6)

This angel is certainly fierce. The sight of him caused Daniel to faint. The angel of the Lord had the same effect on the Roman soldiers who guarded Jesus' tomb—*they shook and became like dead men* when they saw him (Matt. 28:4).

Angels astonish us.

But how do we look to them? Do we seem like small mortal beings that need their protection?

Maybe we look like Jesus to the angels of God—and to the demons of hell, for that matter. In the spiritual realm, we have been fully restored to the image and likeness of God (Col. 3:10), we are clothed in the righteousness of Christ (Isa. 61:10; 1 Cor. 5:21), and we are fully clad in the armor of God (Eph. 6:10-17; Rom. 13:12). We must look so intense standing strong and fully protected from head to toe in our shining armor of light. What if the angels admire us? After all, God loved us enough to send His Son to rescue us, and now we look like a mighty army going out to battle in the Name of the Lord.

But how confusing it must be to these warrior angels when they see us curled up on the floor in the fetal position, whining about how difficult our life has become. They must cringe when they hear us grumbling about our fellow soldiers. They must wince when they see us slinking away from the battle lines against sin. They must pull out their hair by the handfuls (if angels have hair—feathers, maybe?) when we mope about, defeated by the enemy's attacks as if there is nothing we can do about it. They must be thinking, *Pick up your sword, soldier of the Lord, and stand your ground!* They know if we speak even one word of faith from the Sword of the Lord—the Word of God—the enemy instantly will be put to flight.

How easy to forget who we are and where we stand from a spiritual perspective in the ministry of Christian education. Do we approach our assignments in God's kingdom as if we are marching into a battle? Or do we casually and haphazardly approach our tasks without adequate preparation, endangering not only ourselves but also the students who follow us? Are we wearing our armor and wielding our sword of the Spirit?

When I was a US Marine, we were never casual or routine before a mission. We checked and double-checked all our equipment to ensure everything was ready. We never had to search for our weapon—it was with us at all times. How many of us go into our ministry each day unprepared for battle? Can we remember the last time we held up our sword of the Spirit and took our stand? Sadly, some of us may not know where our sword is—we have not seen it in weeks. We must remember we are engaged in battle. Joni Eareckson Tada said,

> This is the only time in history when I get to fight for God. This is the only part of my eternal story when I am actually in the battle. Once I die, I'll be in celebration mode in a glorified body in a whole different set of circumstances. But this is my limited window of opportunity, and I'm going to fight the good fight for all I'm worth.[67]

As Christian school educators, we must remember who we are and what we look like in the spiritual realm because we are fighting for the eternal souls of future generations. To wage this battle, we must do the following:

- Be strong in the Lord in the power of His might.
- Tighten the belt of truth around our waist.
- Fasten the breastplate of righteousness securely on our chest.
- Pull on our boots so we can take the gospel of peace to the whos God places in our life.
- Raise our shields of faith and lock them together with our fellow soldiers to protect ourselves and those entrusted to our care from the evil one's flaming arrows.
- Keep our helmet of salvation firmly positioned on our head, giving us full confidence in the battle.
- Pick up our sword and march boldly into the battle, remembering the victory is already ours because we are more than conquerors through Him! (Eph. 6: 10-17; Rom. 8:37).

Remember that *no weapon that is formed against you will prosper* (Isa. 54:17 NASB). *Greater is he who is in you than he who is in the world* (1 John 4:4 NASB).

# Speak the Very Words of God

*For I have given them the words that you gave me, and they have received them and have come to know in truth that I came from you; and they have believed that you sent me.* John 17:8 (ESV)

Only two things from this world will last forever: the Word of God and the souls of human beings. The greatest joy of participating in Christian school ministry is that we work with both of them every day. Jesus said, *"Heaven and earth will pass away, but my words will never pass away"* (Mark 13:31).

One of my professors at Columbia Bible College, Mary Faith Phillips, drilled this statement into her students: "use every opportunity to say something eternal." Remembering that truth helps me to focus on the whos, and it provides me with a specific strategy for focused action that will make an eternal difference. A Christian educator needs to be:

> … in constant contact with the Book, as every living Christian ought to be; he is actually working with Bible truth, clarifying it in his own mind, seeking to communicate its meaning faithfully and effectively to his pupils. Out of that experience there is bound to come an awareness of the relation of the word of God to his other subjects. Correlation of Christianity with his regular teaching will be natural and intuitive, not forced and calculated.[68]

Hebrews 13:7 is a verse I would like to have engraved on my tombstone: *Remember your leaders, those who spoke to you the word of God. Consider the outcome of their way of life, and imitate their faith* (ESV). I want to be remembered as someone who constantly spoke the Word of God to people. First, I need to apply God's Word to my own heart and life so my faith will be worthy of imitation. I need to love the Lord my God with all my heart, soul, and strength, and keep His commands in my heart. Then I can impress them on others (Deut. 6:5-7). Jesus said that *out of the abundance of the heart [the] mouth speaks* (Luke 6:45 ESV). To speak the Word of God to others, I must first make certain that His word is deep in my own heart. Then with intentionality, I need to speak the Word of God as frequently as possible to those whom I have the opportunity to serve. I call this biblical saturation.

> *For the word of God is living and active, sharper than any two-edged sword, piercing to the division of soul and of spirit, of joints and of marrow, and discerning the thoughts and intentions of the heart.* (Heb. 4:12 ESV)

The turning point in my Christian life was my decision to spend consistent time reading, studying, meditating, and applying the Bible in my daily life. God's Word serves as a cleansing agent, purifying our minds, and allowing us to receive and understand truth (John 15:3; 16:13; 17:17, Eph. 5:26). It can transform our lives, make us wise for salvation through faith in Christ Jesus, and equip us thoroughly for every good work (Rom. 12:2; 2 Tim. 1:15-17).

It is especially important that we not only communicate information about God's Word but also speak *the very words of God* (1 Peter 4:11). Too often, people give their opinion about what the Bible says, but they do not always speak the actual biblical words. These words are God-breathed (2 Tim. 1:16) and are taught by the Spirit of God (1 Cor. 1:13). Jesus said, *"The words I have spoken to you—they are full of the Spirit and life"* (John 6:63). Peter responded to Jesus by saying, *"You have the words of eternal life. We have come to believe and to know that you are the Holy One of God"* (John 6:68-69). Speaking the very words of God allows us to speak directly to the spirit of a person, because we are all created to recognize truth. The best thing a Christian school educator can do to make an eternal difference in the lives of students is to speak the very words of God.

When we focus on a who, we have an opportunity to direct that person's attention toward something eternal. *Faith comes by hearing, and hearing by the word of God* (Rom. 10:17 NKJV). So when we speak the very words of God to others, we help to build their faith, encouraging them to attain a hope *that will not lead to disappointment. For we know how dearly God loves us, because he has given us the Holy Spirit to fill our hearts with his love* (Rom. 5:5 NLT). Therefore, we should always be prepared to give an answer to everyone who asks us for the reason for the hope that resides in us (1 Peter 3:15). And speaking the actual words of God is the best way to give that answer.

We also gain confidence when we speak the Word of God—especially in difficult circumstances. Do you remember what Jesus did when He was tempted by the devil after forty days of fasting in the wilderness? He answered each of the temptations by quoting God's Word (Matt. 4:1-11). Knowing God's Word is crucial so we can speak it *in season and out of season* (2 Tim. 4:2), stand on it, and share it with others as needed.

One of the saddest stories in the Bible is Adam and Eve's temptation in the Garden of Eden. Many people remember only that Eve was beguiled by the serpent; they miss the fact that Adam stood next to her during the temptation (Gen. 3:6). This was the first case—with many to follow—where the enemy took advantage of someone who did not speak the very words of God. God had specifically commanded Adam, *"You are free to eat from any tree in the garden; but you must not eat from the tree of the knowledge of good and evil, for when you eat from it you will certainly die"* (Gen. 2:16-17).

Adam should have memorized these words and communicated them verbatim to Eve—after all, they signified the difference between life and death. Maybe he did. Or maybe some time had passed and God's Word was not as fresh in their minds as it once was. Maybe they had become distracted with too many whats. Whatever the case, when Satan tempted them, he first questioned Eve about God's command: *"Did God really say, 'You must not eat from any tree in the garden'?"* (Gen. 3:1).

But that is not what God had said.

To beguile Eve, Satan slightly reworded God's command and questioned it. This is still his tactic today. Our culture bombards students with similar questions about God's clear commands in Scripture.

Adam should have quoted God's Word with confident authority—the way Jesus did when He was tempted. Maybe Adam's own temptation with the *lust of the flesh, the lust of the eyes, and the pride of life* (1 John 2:16) rendered him complacent and silent. Whatever the reason, he left Eve unprotected from the *devil's schemes* (Eph. 6:11); therefore, she tried to answer the question with her interpretation of God's words. Her paraphrase was close, but she did not speak the very words of God (Gen. 3:3). That proved fatal. Satan then convinced Eve and Adam to rationalize the truth, and they suffered the deadly consequences of sin.

Speaking the very words of God is a matter of life and death for the whos God has entrusted to our care. We must hide God's Word in our hearts, meditate on it, allow it to become our only source of truth, and communicate it verbatim to the next generation. Their lives depend on it. Too often Christian school educators give students a paraphrased version of what God has said. They say, "Children, be nice—Jesus wants us to be nice" instead of saying, *"Be kind and compassionate to one another, forgiving each other, just as in Christ God forgave you"* (Eph. 4:32).

You may say, "But that is the same thing."

No, it is not.

The first statement is good advice based on biblical truth—nothing is necessarily wrong with that. But the second statement is God's exact words. Remember, *the word of God is alive and powerful. It is sharper than the sharpest two-edged sword, cutting between soul and spirit, between joint and marrow. It exposes our innermost thoughts and desires* (Heb. 4:12 NLT). This penetration of God's Word is the means by which the true work of holiness takes place in our lives. We are confronted with our sinfulness and our need to be cleansed through *the washing of water with the word [of God]* (Eph. 5:26 NASB). We then learn how to take our stand in the spiritual battle against unrighteousness. Therefore, our task is to ensure that the word of Christ is dwelling richly in us and in our students (Col. 3:16), providing them with their own *sword of the Spirit* so they will be able to contend effectively for the faith (Eph. 6:17).

> *My child, pay attention to what I say.*
> *Listen carefully to my words.*
> *Don't lose sight of them.*
> *Let them penetrate deep into your heart,*
> *for they bring life to those who find them,*
> *and healing to their whole body.* (Prov. 4:20-22 NLT)

# We Have Come As More Than Conquerors

*My heart has heard you say, "Come and talk with me." And my
heart responds, "LORD, I am coming."* Psalm 27:8 (NLT)

Jane was my friend and colleague in Christian ministry. As an experienced
staff worker, she bailed me out of situations on countless occasions when
I had not planned properly or had failed to communicate important
information in a timely fashion. She was joyful, always humming or
singing—usually songs about Jesus—as she went about her work. Although
her work was demanding and she was often scrambling to meet deadlines,
she was never too busy to stop whatever she was doing to help me. Never.

Cancer rudely interrupted Jane's life when she was still young.
She fought valiantly, temporarily winning her battle when it went into
remission, but within a year, the cancer returned with a vengeance. Her
doctor told her to get her life in order and make her final arrangements,
as she would likely live only a few more months. This kind of news would
bring most of us to our knees. But not Jane. She became quite excited
and prepared for those last months as if she had won an all-expenses-paid
vacation to an exotic destination.

In fact, she had.

The last time I saw my friend, she had come to the school to tell us
about her journey and to bid us farewell. With many tears and gentle hugs,
along with much sadness, we embraced her once boundless and energetic
body, which had become a frail image of its former self. But she did not
come to mourn or to grieve. She came to celebrate with us; she wanted us
to share her enthusiasm about her destination. After sharing what God had
been teaching her, she asked if she could pray for us.

Pray for us? I thought. We should be all be praying for her.

As we huddled around her to hear her feeble voice, she sat straighter in
her chair and said enthusiastically, "We are about to bow our heads, close
our eyes, and talk to Jesus right now. But guess what? I might actually get
to see Him today!"

I could not hear what Jane prayed that day because I was overwhelmed
with my own tears—tears of deep admiration for this woman who faced
her greatest challenge with such confidence and joy, as well as tears of

repentance that I had allowed my own prayer life to become a numb, religious activity instead of a close walk with my Friend and Savior.

Jane had her eyes fixed on Who.

A few days later, her wish was granted.

Can you envision your entrance into eternity? John Bunyan paints this picture in *Pilgrim's Progress* when Christian entered the Celestial City:

> There came out also at this time, to meet them, several of the King's trumpeters, clothed in white and shining raiment; who, with melodious noises, and loud, made even the heavens to echo with their sound. These trumpeters saluted Christian and his fellow with ten thousand welcomes, from the world: and this they did with shouting and sound of trumpet. This done, they compassed them round on every side... continually sounding as they went, with melodious noise, in notes on high; so that the very sight was, to them that could behold it, as if heaven itself was come down to meet them. Thus, therefore, they walked on together; and as they walked, ever and anon these trumpeters, even, with joyful sound, would, by mixing their music with looks and gestures, still signify to Christian and his brother how welcome they were into their company, and with what gladness they came to meet them.... Oh, by what tongue or pen can their glorious joy be expressed![69]

The author of Hebrews gives this extraordinary description:

> *But you have come to Mount Zion, to the city of the living God, the heavenly Jerusalem. You have come to thousands of angels gathered together with joy. You have come to the meeting of God's firstborn children whose names are written in heaven. You have come to God, the judge of all people, and to the spirits of good people who have been made perfect. You have come to Jesus, the One who brought the new agreement from God to his people, and you have come to the sprinkled*

*blood that has a better message than the blood of Abel.... So
let us be thankful, because we have a kingdom that cannot
be shaken.* (Heb. 12:22-24, 28 NCV)

This encouraging passage strengthens me. What courage. What fearlessness!
Slow down and picture in your minds what we have come to:

- The city of the Living God (Mount Zion, the heavenly Jerusalem)
- Thousands of angels gathered in joyful celebration
- The meeting of God's firstborn children whose names are written in heaven
- God, the judge of all people
- The spirits of good people who have been made perfect
- Jesus, the Mediator of the New Covenant
- Sprinkled blood (better than Abel's)
- A kingdom that cannot be shaken

Do not miss the amazing truth of this passage: we have already come.

While we will experience the full reality of this in heaven, we have already arrived there spiritually. Imagine what our service in Christian ministry would look like if we approached it from this understanding. What if we came to our ministries mindful that we are clothed in Jesus' righteousness, prepared for battle in our armor of light, and speaking the very words of God? What if we were mindful of the *great cloud of witnesses* that surrounds us—the Living God, the Judge of all the earth, thousands of angels, and all God's children made perfect in Christ by His sprinkled blood of the new covenant in an unshakable kingdom (Heb. 12:3)? Imagine what we could accomplish.

> God is infinite. He can do and have whatever He wants. Yet, incredibly, He desires fellowship with finite, flawed human beings. The magnitude of His character greatly exceeds anything we can possibly comprehend. Moreover, although He has myriads of angels and heavenly creatures eager to immediately do His bidding, God still chooses to work through people. It is unfathomable.[70]

In addition to all these astonishing resources of heaven at our disposal, Jesus also fills us with His Holy Spirit to empower us to be more than conquerors through His unending love as we serve in His unshakable kingdom (Rom. 5:5; 8:37-39). Consider J. Oswald Sanders's description of this:

> To be filled with the Spirit means simply that the Christian voluntarily surrenders life and will to the Spirit. Through faith, the believer's personality is filled, mastered, and controlled by the Spirit. The meaning of "filled" is not "to pour into a passive container" but to "take possession of the mind." When we invite the Spirit to fill us, the Spirit's power grips our lives with this kind of strength and passion.[71]

The Holy Spirit empowers us with the same power that raised Jesus from the dead (Rom. 8:11), strengthens us to serve God beyond our own limitations and weaknesses (Eph. 3:16), and transforms us into conquering kingdom warriors. It is time to wage the battle for the souls of those entrusted to our care in the power of the Holy Spirit. Meditate on this description of Hudson Taylor, a missionary in China for more than fifty years:

> A man full of faith and the Holy Ghost, of entire surrender to God and His call, of great self-denial, heartfelt compassion, rare power in prayer, marvelous organizing faculty, indefatigable perseverance, and of astounding influence with men, and withal of childlike simplicity himself.[72]

This is what it takes to be effective in Christian ministry. We must be full of the Holy Spirit to experience the victory that is already ours. And we must continually empty ourselves of our own strength and self-sufficiency, being surrendered to His control and transformed by His power in order to be used in the transformation of others.

> *Don't grieve God. Don't break his heart. His Holy Spirit, moving and breathing in you, is the most intimate part of your life, making you fit for himself. Don't take such a gift for granted.* (Eph. 4:30 MSG)

Here is a challenge for each of us who have been called to the ministry of Christian education: Instead of being timid about the ministry of Christian education, we should be bold. Instead of complaining about challenges and difficulties, we should remember we have already come to an unshakable kingdom. And, like my friend Jane, we should rejoice. We may see Jesus today!

# Preparing Our Students

*There is always one moment in childhood when*
*the door opens and lets the future in.*
Graham Greene [73]

The future.

Christianity always stands confidently on the past as it leans forward toward the future—specifically, the future glory of God's eternal kingdom. The immediate future for us as Christian educators is our focus on the next generation. The psalmist wrote, *We will tell the next generation the praiseworthy deeds of the LORD, his power, and the wonders he has done* (Ps. 78:4). We will know we have done this correctly when future generations put their trust in God, remember what He has done, and keep His commands (Ps. 78:7). For this to happen, our students need to be adequately prepared to focus on Who (and who). Jeff Myers says,

> In a relay race, the responsibility for the one passing the baton falls to the one who is carrying it, not to the one who is receiving it. An entire generation is looking to you to lift their eyes to a higher goal—a life of character, friendship and community, a life that grows richer by giving rather than by getting.[74]

Microscopes, telescopes, binoculars, sighting scopes, and eyeglasses help us see something more clearly—magnified and focused for a purpose. So what is the purpose of focusing on the whos? Discipleship. Jesus has called us to make disciples (Matt. 28:19).

What is our role as Christian educators in the disciple-making process? What is our focus? First, remember that God has given parents the responsibility of nurturing their children in spiritual matters (Deut. 6:4-7). Christian educators have been granted the privilege and opportunity to partner with parents in the discipleship of their children. This collective discipleship—a collaborative effort between Christian parents, pastors, teachers, support staff, and coaches—links the home, church, and school together to produce an environment conducive for spiritual formation.

Our combined goal is to produce disciples for Jesus Christ, equipping them to follow Jesus and to make disciples for the rest of their lives. We want students to honor and please the Lord, producing every kind of good fruit as they grow in the knowledge of God (Col. 1:6-10; Matt. 28:19; John 15:8).

One year, when our three children were all in middle and high school, I counted thirty-eight people in our church and Christian school (pastors, teachers, support staff, and coaches) who had significant daily or weekly direct contact with them. I was overwhelmed with joy when I calculated the potential for spiritual growth in my children through the united efforts of these godly people who were committed to discipleship. To this day, I see the spiritual impact of these individuals and countless others who helped us bring up our children in the *training and instruction of the Lord* (Eph. 6:4).

In a Christian school, opportunities abound for discipleship both during instruction and through extracurricular activities. In the natural ebb and flow of school life—in the classroom, on the playground, or through participation in the arts or athletics—students experience the opportunities to apply biblical truth to their lives in an environment rich with potential for spiritual formation.

Spiritual formation, a synonym for spiritual growth or sanctification, is the process of Christ being fully developed in us, fostered by the work of the Holy Spirit within the context of discipleship relationships (Gal. 4:19). Paul writes, *And we all, who with unveiled faces contemplate [or behold] the Lord's glory, are being transformed into his image with ever-increasing glory, which comes from the Lord, who is the Spirit* (2 Cor. 3:18). The Holy Spirit, living within believers (Rom. 8:9-11; 1 Cor. 3:16), is working to transform, empower, and equip them for godly living and effective Christian service (Gal. 5:22-23; Rom. 12:1-8). An essential component for discipleship in a Christian school is the tangible presence of the Holy Spirit in the educational process. True discipleship always begins with the gospel message of new life in Jesus Christ, then moves on naturally to the process of spiritual growth culminating in ever-increasing victorious Christian living. This takes place when godly Christian educators are empowered by the Holy Spirit to model and speak the truth from God's Word into the lives of their students.

The Bible is the most important book in a Christian school. Every day our students are learning to hear and recognize the voice of God through a biblically infused curriculum in a relational setting with godly Christian educators. We should follow Paul's instructions to Timothy to *preach the Good News. Be ready at all times, and tell people what they need to do. Tell them when they are wrong. Encourage them with great patience and careful teaching* (2 Tim. 4:2 NCV). Glen Schultz says,

> Regardless of the name that is on any school entrance, kingdom education only takes place where God's Word is central to all instruction. It only takes place where the teachers think and act from a biblical worldview, and this can happen only when the teacher studies the Word as much as he or she studies the subject being taught.[75]

But Christian education should also include more than the teaching of the Bible. Every academic subject in the teaching and learning process is important and becomes a natural opportunity for biblical integration. The study of science, history, language, or mathematics is an opportunity to understand more fully God's creation and our place in it. In fact, the best way to understand *God's invisible qualities—His eternal power and divine nature*—is to study what He has created (Rom. 1:20). Therefore, academic excellence is a natural by-product of a Christ-centered education. Christians have a significant reason to study: if we understand God and His creation more fully, we will more be effective in the building of His kingdom. During their Babylonian captivity, God gave Daniel and his three Hebrew friends *knowledge and understanding of all kinds of literature and learning… wisdom and understanding … ten times better than all the magicians and enchanters in the whole kingdom* (Dan. 1:17, 20). Richard Riesen says,

> Christian educators must engage the world intellectually, even at the cutting edge. Far from enervating our interest in academic work, our faith ought to inflame it. That should be the message students are getting in Christian schools: There is no such thing as Christian education that is too academic.[76]

People sometimes ask me, "What do you value most about a Christian education—spiritual formation or academic preparation?" My answer is both. I do not see these two things as separate. One demands the other. And in the ministry of Christian education, both are simultaneously achieved through a biblically infused teaching and learning process. Academic preparation alone, without spiritual formation, is not enough. *The wisdom of this world is foolishness in God's sight* (1 Cor. 3:19). Our students need the power of the Holy Spirit working in their lives so they can live holy lives of effective Christian service. But spiritual formation that is missing the academic necessities to serve God as an ambassador to the world is also ineffective. We know that *Jesus grew in wisdom and stature, and in favor with God and man* (Luke 2:52). He was greatly respected by those who followed Him because of His knowledge and His spiritual capabilities. Many of God's servants in the Bible were carefully prepared academically and spiritually to accomplish what He called them to do.

Our role of discipleship as Christian educators takes place at the intersection of what God says to us, what God says to our students, and what their circumstances are. At that intersection, the Holy Spirit works to accomplish spiritual growth and development. There, our compassion and attentiveness can be tools in God's hand to produce spiritual transformation. Dan Egeler says,

> Each of us can be a mentor. The role doesn't necessarily entail spending your life in Africa or even as a full-time teacher or coach—it may just take a small act of kindness that the Holy Spirit can turn into a powerful force in the life of a young person. Such is the hallmark of a mentor.[77]

Sadly, sometimes we are so busy in ministry that we do not focus on our students—we do not see their circumstances, hear what God is saying to them, and take action on their behalf. We may need to bolster their faith, encourage their commitment, rescue them from the pit of sinful consequences, restore them to full strength, inspire them to renewed hope, or equip them in some specific way to be effective disciples of Jesus Christ. To be successful in passing on our faith to the next generation, we must carefully consider our responsibility to pass on the truth with which we have been entrusted to trustworthy young men and women who will also be able to teach it to others (2 Tim. 2:2). But we must be aware of our enemy; his goal is to prevent us from doing that:

> Given Satan's single-minded purpose—destroy God and rule the universe—we can count on him to put his most destructive resources into play at the front lines of the eternal battle against God. Where are those front lines? In the minds, hearts, and souls of children. Ever the strategic mastermind, Satan knows well that if you destroy the character and hope of children, you rule the world! Satan is not omnipotent, but he is intelligent and clever—certainly sharp enough to realize that if you win over children, you have won the war for at least one generation and probably more.[78]

We are engaged in a battle—a battle for the hearts and minds of the next generation. How can we tell if we are winning this battle? The answer can be found in our students' eyes. On what are they focused? Are they focused on whos or are they focused on whats? Here is a sobering thought: *the student is not above the teacher, but everyone who is fully trained will be like their teacher* (Luke 6:40). Are we truly discipling them—effectively modeling and training our students to know how to focus on whos and not whats?

As the disciples watched Jesus ascend to heaven, two angels asked them, *"Why do you stand here looking into the sky? This same Jesus, who has been taken from you into heaven, will come back in the same way you have seen him go into heaven"* (Acts 1:11). The disciples had learned to keep their eyes fixed on Jesus; they were looking intently at Him until He was completely out of sight. Then they turned their focus toward the whos in Jerusalem, Judea, Samaria, and the ends of the earth (Acts 1:8).

Now it is our turn.

# CHAPTER 9

# Follow the Eyes of Jesus Again

*The eyes are the window of the soul.* English Proverb

Look into another person's eyes, and you can see pain, fear, excitement, disappointment, anticipation, love, rage, or even contentment. Of course, people can avoid eye contact or stare in another direction to prevent others from looking into their souls. But most of the time, we rely on body language—especially eye contact—to understand what another person believes and is trying to communicate.

Following the eyes of Jesus through what is revealed in God's Word helps us to understand His focus more fully and becomes a model for our focus in life and ministry. Sometimes the gospel writers gave us specific descriptions about who and what Jesus was looking at. Other times, we have to use our holy imagination to see what may have been reflected in Jesus' eyes. In either case, if we follow the eyes of Jesus, we will improve our focus and serve Him more effectively.

The first thing I notice when I try to see the eyes of Jesus is that they are lifted toward heaven as He communed with His heavenly Father in prayer. He often withdrew to lonely places to spend time with His Father (Luke 5:16; 6:12). Jesus lifted His eyes to heaven when He prayed in public before breaking bread, as He was healing someone, or when He prayed for His disciples (Mark 6:41, 7:34; John 17:1). He also lifted His eyes to heaven as He talked with His Father outside of Lazarus's tomb before He ' raised him from the dead (John 11:41). Clearly, Jesus was intently focused on His Father to accomplish His will for His glory.

But Jesus' eyes were not always lifted up in prayer. In the Garden of Gethsemane, He knelt in prayer with His head down on the ground under the terrible weight of what He faced (Matt. 26:39). Likewise, from the agony of Golgotha's cross, He cried out to His Father, with His eyes looking down on those who crucified Him, interceding for their forgiveness (Luke 23:34). Can you see His eyes bowed low under the dreadful reality that His Father had forsaken Him as He bore the sins of the world? (Matt. 27:46; 1 Peter 2:24). Then His eyes were closed in death and burial in the garden tomb.

Can you imagine the moment Jesus opened His eyes as He rose from the dead? Once again, He focused on His heavenly Father (John 16:17). Then we see Jesus' eyes trained on His disciples for forty days as He prepared them for their role in the Great Commission (Matt. 28:19-20; Acts 1:3). We do not know whether Jesus was looking up into heaven as He ascended or whether He was looking down on His disciples (Acts 1:9). He may have done both. Now He lives to make intercession for us at the right hand of His Father (Heb. 7:25; Rom. 8:24), His eyes eternally focused on Who (and who).

Jesus provides us with a perfect model of how to focus on Who. And because His focus was so constant, He could see His Father's merciful eyes of compassion directed toward the objects of His great love—us. Watch Jesus' eyes as you read the gospel accounts. He is always searching the crowd to find someone who is lost, broken, afraid, or desperate. Note what Luke said in his description of the widow of Nain as she walked in the funeral procession of her only son: *when the Lord saw her, his heart overflowed with compassion* (Luke 7:13 NLT). Out of this heart of compassion, Jesus raised her son from the dead. The same was true for the woman who pressed through the crowd to touch the hem of His garment. *When Jesus saw her, he called her forward* and proclaimed her healing and freedom from the bondage of Satan (Luke 13:12). Or how about the man by the pool of Bethesda who had been sick for thirty-eight years? *When Jesus saw him lying there,* He healed him (John 5:6). Clearly, Jesus was doing the work of His Father on our behalf. Early in His ministry, Jesus said, *"I have come down from heaven not to do my will but to do the will of him who sent me"* (John 6:38). He was true to this commitment to the end, dedicating Himself to accept His Father's will on the night He was betrayed. Jesus embraced fully His Father's mission *to seek and to save the lost* (Luke 19:10).

Jesus, therefore, is a wonderful example for us. He always focused on His Father and on the needy people He encountered. Circumstances and material things did not distract Him. He was God-focused and people-focused. His eyes were focused on the whos all the way to the cross, where He gave His life as a ransom for many—an indescribable gift of love to the world (2 Cor. 9:15). Through all this, I see His eyes intently focused on me.

To be effective, Christian school educators also need to be God-focused and people-focused. We too easily lose our focus in ministry by working on the important tasks and building the important resources, while slowly losing sight of Who (and who) we are serving.

This leads me to ask, "Where are my eyes focused?" Are they focused intently on my heavenly Father and on His Son, the Lord Jesus Christ? Are they focused intently on the cross and empty tomb (Gal. 2:20, 6:14; Rom. 6:5-10)? Are they focused intently on the other whos He came to save? Do my eyes communicate love, compassion, and reassurance? Do my eyes reveal my desire for others to know the truth, to walk in the light, to experience and share His love, and to receive eternal, abundant life?

When Jesus healed the man born blind (and note John says Jesus *saw* this blind man), the healed man's testimony to the Pharisees who questioned Him was, *"One thing I do know. I was blind but now I see!"* (John 9:25). Like this man, we were born in spiritual blindness. We did not have the capability to focus on Who. But Jesus gave us sight. He said, *"I am the light of the world. If you follow me, you won't have to walk in darkness, because you will have the light that leads to life"* (John 8:12 NLT).

I desperately want to see others the way Jesus sees them. He notices them. He is looking for them. This is the sincere prayer of my heart, and I hope it will be your prayer as well: "Lord, please heal me of my self-centered blindness so I can focus intently on You and focus intently on the whos You have graciously placed in my life to serve."

> The example Jesus set should motivate us to live the life He has called us to live. He is waiting for us to realize the passions, abilities, and dreams He has set in place for us so on that day when we are told "well done, my good and faithful servant," we will know exactly why He is congratulating us. Let's live that life.[79]

# CHAPTER 10

# Go to the Other Side Again

*[Jesus] answered, "You give them something to eat."* Mark 6:37

The crowds had once again followed Jesus when He attempted to retreat privately by boat to a solitary place to get some rest with His disciples. Yet He had compassion on these people because they were like *sheep without a shepherd* (Matt. 9:36). He loved them, healed them, and taught them many things about the Kingdom of God. As evening approached, the disciples tried to persuade Jesus to send away the crowds so they could buy themselves some food to eat. But instead, Jesus told His disciples to feed them. How could they? More than 5,000 people had gathered there.

This was a major lesson for Jesus' disciples. He was teaching them to see people through His eyes of compassion and to meet their needs—with His power, not their own. He was teaching them to see the people (the whos) right in front of them. Jesus multiplied the bread and fish, but the disciples gave it to the people to eat. They were feeding the sheep.

Jesus still says that to His disciples: *feed my sheep* (John 21:17). We are responsible for many little lambs as His servants in Christian school ministry. He has great compassion on all of them, and He wants us to meet their needs. Of course, He will provide their spiritual food—the Word of God. He will multiply it in our hands so we can feed them, which is the reason biblical integration is so important. Jesus said, *"Man shall not live on bread alone but on every word that comes from the mouth of God"* (Matt. 4:4).

Our students need God's Word for their spiritual growth and development. 1 Peter 2:2-3 says, *Like newborn babies, crave pure spiritual milk, so that by it you may grow up in your salvation, now that you have tasted that the Lord is good.* They need God's Word as their *sword of the Spirit* (Eph. 6:17) in the battles they will fight. We are privileged to provide baskets full of truth for our students' nourishment and enablement as Jesus provides it in our hearts and minds.

Immediately following the feeding of the 5,000, as the disciples were still carrying baskets full of leftover pieces of bread and fish, Jesus told them for a second time to get into the boat and go ahead of Him to the other side of the Sea of Galilee (Matt. 14:22). Can you imagine the stir this created among the disciples? They were probably still overwhelmed and excited by the miracle that had just occurred in their hands. Yet they also were likely perplexed that Jesus was not going with them in the boat. Who would protect Him while He was alone on the mountainside at night? Did they discuss what had taken place the last time Jesus said, *"Let us go to the other side"*—especially when a strong wind caused the waves to buffet them? Once again, they found themselves straining against the oars—only this time, Jesus was not present.

But He *was* with them.

He was not in the boat with them; He was walking beside it on the water!

Initially, the disciples did not recognize Him. They thought He was a ghost. Going to the other side seemed to be a bad idea every time. But Jesus interrupted their terror and said, *"Take courage. It is I. Don't be afraid"* (Matt. 14:27). Peter instantly believed, and he alone had the courage to come to Jesus on the water when He summoned him. Although his faith was short-lived, Peter experienced the miracle of walking on the water with Jesus because of his willingness to take a giant step of faith. As long as he focused on Jesus, he was able to walk on the water, but when he saw the waves, he lost his focus on Who. The other disciples were bewildered and amazed by what they witnessed. And when Jesus stepped into the boat, the wind died down. Surely, they remembered His previous proclamation, *"Peace, be still"* (Mark 4:39 NKJV).

And this time they responded without fear. They worshiped Him saying, *"Truly you are the Son of God"* (Matt. 14:33). Quite an improvement since their previous trip to the other side!

*When they had crossed over, they landed at Gennesaret* (Matt. 14:34). Can you imagine their absolute wonder and confusion over what had just occurred? They were supposed to be landing at Bethsaida (Mark 6:45), but the storm had redirected them once again to the region of the Decapolis. Jesus had returned them to the place of His eternal focus, where more than 4,000 believers gathered with their missionary, formerly known as the demon-possessed man. This was the result of Jesus' earlier seed planting. Throughout the region, this man had told his story about what Jesus had done for him and the mercy He had shown him. Then Jesus and His disciples immediately went to work healing them and feeding them (Mark 7:31-8:13; Matt. 15:29-39).

In this account, the disciples focused on Who—Jesus. And when they recognized and worshiped Him, they were able to focus on the whos He had come to serve. Like the disciples, our role is to bring Jesus to others so He can minister to them. Perhaps during the storms of difficulty we face as we are *straining at the oars* with the wind against us and buffeted by the waves, we will see Jesus coming to our rescue. Like Peter, we may not always get it exactly right, but when our sincere desire is to be with Jesus, to place our focus completely on Him, He will say, "Come." When He steps into the storms of our lives and calms the wind blowing against us, then we can join Him in His work and minister to the whos before us.

Do you recognize Him? Can you hear Him say, "Come," as you focus your attention on Him? Are you ready to take active steps of faith to draw close to Him, even if you fail, knowing He will never leave you or forsake you? Do you feel the calm—His *"Peace, be still"*—when He enters your situation? Do you worship Him as the Son of God? Do you see clearly, with eyes of faith, the destination He has chosen for you—the who—and the potential in that who to impact thousands of other whos for the Kingdom of God?

Let us go to the other side.

## CHAPTER 11

# A True Story of Clear Focus

*Go into all the world and preach the Good
News to everyone.* Mark 16:15 (NLT)

"Luwak coffee?" our taxi driver asked. "Have you heard of it?"

Little did I know that this question would be the most significant of
the day—a day filled with going place to place in an Indonesian artists'
market. Talented silversmiths crafted one-of-a-kind jewelry, wood-carvers
sculpted three-dimensional masterpieces from a single piece of sandalwood,
and painters recreated beautiful scenes from Indonesian life on canvas. On
any other day, it would have been the opportunity of a lifetime. But the
crowded stop-and-go traffic combined with the strong incense smoke
offered up to the Hindu gods, which filled the breathable air in the market
shops, brought on a lightheaded nausea in my stomach. In one particular
shop, I sensed a strong spiritual attack. I silently prayed as I left the shop,
"Greater is He that is in me than he that is in the world." But as my nausea
increased, I simply wanted to go to the hotel and rest.

Although my wife, Melanie, and I had been in Indonesia for less than a
week, we were feeling somewhat adventurous. We had survived the twenty-
seven hour airplane trip from South Carolina to arrive on the other side of
the world, where we had been invited to participate in several opportunities
to encourage Christian school educators in the Pacific Rim region of Asia.
Our host had met us near the airport and had given us a cell phone in
case we needed assistance. So far, the only thing we had done with the

cell phone was to hold it up beside a traffic circle one evening on our way to dinner, using the light from the phone display to hail a cab. It worked, and our new friend and taxi driver, Mani, offered to take us shopping on the following day. The journey included stops in various markets along a three-hour route. We did not realize at the time that God was orchestrating our "chance" meeting with this particular driver.

On the drive to the market, we passed dozens of Hindu temples, makeshift shops and restaurants, and hundreds of motorcycles (the preferred and most economical mode of travel in Indonesia)—some with entire families huddled on them. We passed beautiful rice fields with the field workers bent over, their conical bamboo hats shading them from the hot Indonesian sun that beat mercilessly down on them. I marveled at the interesting juxtaposition of a worker talking on a cell phone while he held the handmade rice harvesting tools of yesteryear.

Another sudden stop in traffic brought me back to reality.

"Luwak coffee?" Mani asked with a grin. His question pierced the mental and spiritual malaise I was experiencing.

"No thank you," I responded.

"Luwak coffee—you know it?" Mani pressed.

"Yes, but not right now," I said.

I knew about Luwak coffee, and honestly, it was the last thing in the world I wanted to drink in my nauseated condition. Kopi Luwak was popularized in the 2007 movie, *The Bucket List*, starring Jack Nicholson and Morgan Freeman. Touted as the most rare and most expensive coffee in the world, this Indonesian delicacy can cost as much as $50 per cup in gourmet coffee establishments in London or New York City. Its cost is related to the unique way the coffee beans are processed to reduce their acidity. I will spare you the details, but the process involves a civet (a catlike animal called a Luwak in the Indonesian language) eating the coffee beans, then twelve hours later … need I say more?

A friend from Indonesia had introduced me to Luwak coffee almost one year earlier. It is delicious—if you can get past its source. But you have to be in the right frame of mind to enjoy such a luxury. So I declined Mani's offer.

But Mani was persistent. "You need to go to this Luwak coffee plantation!"

When he realized I was about to decline a third time (the Indonesian equivalent to "absolutely not"), he quickly said with a childlike grin, "They have the animal—the Luwak."

Somehow, Mani had detected my inability to resist such a boyish opportunity. If the coffee was the most rare coffee in the world, how much more rare was the animal? Carsick or not, I could not resist.

"Yes," I said. "We'll go to the Luwak Coffee Plantation."

Mani explained that we would be able to see the entire Luwak coffee production from the beans on the tree all the way to drinking a freshly roasted and hand-ground cup of Kopi Luwak. Again, I silently asked the Lord to help me overcome my sickness and what seemed like some kind of spiritual attack. Still I searched for my camera with excited anticipation. I had no idea that Melanie and I were about to encounter something that would change the rest of our lives.

"Hello, Ma'am and Sir. Please allow me to introduce myself. I am Rio and I will be your guide at Luwak Coffee Plantation today."

Rio was a tall, slender young man with a contagious smile and confident energy. He delievered his well-rehearsed, best-English speech with pride and many smiles. Yet his unwashed clothing indicated that he was not among the privileged of this society. Nevertheless, he carried himself resolutely as if he owned the plantation. We made small talk as Rio took us on the tour, explaining the difference between various coffee trees and their beans. Along the way, he asked us questions about our home and family. He wanted to know more about our children, which as it turned out, were similar in age to him. He was twenty-two years old, married, and the father of a seven-month-old—something he called his MBA—married by accident. Although he made light of it, his eyes reflected the pain of this "accident" as well as his willingness to own it and be an honorable man to his wife and son.

We saw the coffee beans that had been harvested, and we smelled them being roasted over an open wood fire. We also saw the civet along the pathway leading through the plantation. It was curled up asleep in a hollow log in its cage. We learned from Rio that civets are nocturnal animals, so they sleep all day. He gently attempted to wake the sleeping animal, but we elected to let it rest, only taking a picture of it in the hollow log. If I had known it would be asleep, I would have passed on the visit to the coffee plantation. Near the end of the tour, we helped an elderly woman pound the beans into a powder with a heavy stick. This powder was then added to hot water to make a fresh cup of Luwak coffee for us to enjoy.

Rio invited us to sit down at an old, dilapidated wooden table that was positioned to overlook the valley down below. In the distance, I heard the mournful sound of the Muslim call to prayer. Competing with it was the tinkling sound of a Hindu wind chime hanging loosely in a nearby tree. I thought it odd that both sounds seemed to be vying for our attention at that particular moment.

Rio sat across from us while a young girl served us a steaming cup of Kopi Luwak. She also placed a serving tray on the table containing six small cups of additional coffee samples for us to try. Rio described each sample, hoping we would purchase some coffee in the gift shop. Then, instead of talking about coffee, Rio talked about his life.

"My life is like this Luwak coffee—sh—coffee." He said softly and with a sense of reflection.

This was a rather abrupt and unexpected "sales pitch," but Rio's eyes indicated that he was holding in some major emotional pain and his comedic comments were intended to mask it.

"Things are starting to get better for me now since my wife has been teaching me about Karma. Now I have this good job as a tour guide, and I get to meet nice people like you," he said with a forced smile.

"I don't know why I am telling you all of this," he continued.

"Please, go on," I urged, sensing this young man was reaching out to us for help.

Rio became increasingly more transparent as he talked, describing his early life as an orphan who never knew his mother or father, growing up on the streets begging for money, and trying to survive any way he could. He said that at times he had done shameful things such as stealing money. His eyes filled with tears as he told us he had never been able to go to school but was trying to teach himself to read. I sensed in my spirit that he was a very lonely young man who needed to belong to someone. He was obviously searching for truth, longing for purpose, and yearning for significance. Where could he find these as a pitiful orphan in a spiritually oppressed land filled with false gods?

Rio took a big breath and wiped the tears from his eyes. He apologized for his embarrassing conversation. I told him that it was okay and that we wanted to hear his story. Only the day before, I had read Mike Nappa's *God in Slow Motion*. The theme of the book seemed to be that God is a very compassionate God. He listens—really listens to us—and meets us at our point of desperation. Then He gives us His strength as His response. Reading that book had prepared me specifically for this God-ordained conversation.

Tears flowed. Were they stored-up tears of a little boy desperately searching the streets of Indonesia for his father and mother? Were they tears of unmet anguish of soul and unresolved grief, longing for unconditional love and approval? Or were they tears of regret, shame, and a lifetime of disappointment? So many tears.

"I really don't know why I am telling you all of this!" Rio exclaimed. "I have tried my whole life to know who I am and why I am here."

Our hearts were moved to compassion for this young man. We realized that he was the who in a day filled with many whats. The best thing we could do was to focus on him.

Then suddenly, in an act of desperation, Rio, with tears streaming down his face, held up his hands and said emphatically, "I just want to know who created me! I don't know my mother and my father, but maybe someday they will want to find me."

I realized that was my cue. The reason God had orchestrated all the events in our lives to bring us to Indonesia, to this exact place at this exact time became crystal clear.

"Rio," I said, "I know who created you."

He was visibly shocked and replied, "You do? You know my parents?"

"I don't know your parents, but I do know who created you," I quickly clarified. "God, the Creator of everything, made you. He loves you and He promises to be a Father to the one who does not have a father."

Rio, still wiping tears from his eyes responded, "How do you know this?"

"God told us in His book—the Bible. Do you know about the Bible?" I asked.

Rio had never heard anything about God, the Bible, or Jesus. He asked if they were part of Karma. I explained that Karma was an idea, but that

Jesus is a person—God's Son who came to earth to rescue us from our broken lives, and He wants to have a relationship with us.

Rio asked, "Can I meet Him? I never knew I could know my God in person."

"Oh yes, Rio. You can meet Him," I replied.

At that instant, large gusts of wind began to blow. Each gust seemed to blow the sound of the Muslim call to prayer louder and louder, making it difficult to talk with Rio. Simultaneously, the Hindu wind chime in the nearby tree spun feverishly, round and round, its bells ringing louder and louder.

We were in the midst of a spiritual battle for Rio's heart and mind. Everything about the day made sense—the spiritual attack in the market, the nausea from the incense, and the wind and noise. All of it was the enemy's attempt to distract me.

I prayed aloud for Rio—that he would be able to understand how to meet his God, how to receive Jesus as his Savior, and how to have a new life. As I prayed, the wind grew even stronger, drowning out the call to prayer and nearly breaking the wind chime. But this wind was different—a rushing, mighty wind of the Holy Spirit that blew through and removed all distractions. Then suddenly the wind stopped. Everything became quiet and calm.

In that exceedingly peaceful moment, I asked Rio if he would like to pray to his heavenly Father and meet Jesus—the One who could give him a new life. He said yes, but he sadly explained that he did not know how to pray—no one had taught him. I reached across the Luwak coffee table, took his hand, and placed it in Melanie's hand. I said, "When children are little, their mothers teach them how to pray. Melanie will now be your mother and she will teach you how to pray."

He smiled and agreed.

What happened next was simply too beautiful to describe. A mother's tear-soaked voice praying the most simple, childlike prayer, echoed line-by-line by a little boy's heartfelt response. Soon Rio's words became his own cry to his Father.

"God, I want to know you. I've been looking for you all my life, and now you have found me."

We were no longer sitting at a Luwak coffee table. We sat at a communion table, and our new spiritual son was being filled with the Holy Spirit right before our eyes.

Tears flowed. A river of tears. But these were tears of joy, shed by one who finally had found shelter in the loving arms of Jesus. These tears came from one who had discovered the comfort and security of belonging—adopted by an eternal Father who will never disappoint him. These tears signaled freedom from fear and doubt—tears of a much-loved son.

"I am a child of God!" Rio exclaimed triumphantly. His smile beamed radiantly as a new creation in Christ.

"Right," I agreed. "And from now on, you have a Father who promises to never leave you." Then I took Rio's hand and said, "I also want you to know that you now have an earthly father and mother—you are our son."

Rio's smile grew brighter and brighter. At that moment, he sat straight up, held both of his hands to his chest, and looked down toward his heart.

"It is quiet inside," he said. "I've never felt this before."

A sweet peace enveloped the three of us as we enjoyed the presence of the Lord. An indescribable joy cascaded on us as we experienced the eternal love of our heavenly Father. With the eagerness of a child, Rio's first action as a new believer was to jump up and exclaim, "I can't wait to tell my wife about all of this!"

In the days and weeks following that amazing experience, we shared many conversations with Rio. We, along with other Indonesian believers, experienced the wonderful blessing of discipling Rio and helping him learn how to follow Jesus. He is growing rapidly in his new faith, and he is already telling others about Jesus too.

Rio is a who! He is such an important who that God called us to go to the other side of the world to tell him about his heavenly Father, the One he had searched for his entire life. He brought us to tell him about the One who created him, who loved him so much that He sent Jesus to rescue him.

Jesus' eyes have always been focused on Rio.

By God's grace, He enabled us to focus on Rio too.

And now Rio is focusing on Who (and who).

# CONCLUSION

Who is in your focus? Is it Jesus? Is He truly the most significant person in your life and ministry? Or, has the tyranny of all the whats replaced Him?

Can you see His eyes looking at the Rios in your life, longing for them to come and sit at His feet to receive His loving mercy and grace? Are you ready to help bring in the harvest from His fields?

Right now, in the quiet of this moment, I urge you to allow the Holy Spirit to help you rediscover the most important aspect of Christian school ministry:

A clear focus.

# ENDNOTES

1   Shane Kindschi, http://www.kindschi.com/

2   "Turn Your Eyes Upon Jesus: The Song and the Story," http://www.sharefaith. com/guide/Christian-Music/hymns-the-songs-and-the-stories/turn-your-eyes-upon-jesus-the-song-and-the-story.html (accessed: March 20, 2015).

3   Mike Nappa, *God in Slow Motion: Reflections on Jesus and the 10 Unexpected Lessons You Can See in His Life* (Nashville, TN: Thomas Nelson, 2013), 60-61.

4   Kenneth Coley, *Navigating the Storms: Leading Christian Schools with Character and Conviction* (Colorado Springs, CO: Purposeful Design), 66.

5   Note: A legion was a Roman regiment of 6,000 soldiers—William Barclay, *The Gospel of Luke*, Daily Bible Study Series (Philadelphia, PA: Westminster Press, 1975), 108.

6   William Barclay, *The Gospel of Luke*, Daily Bible Study Series (Philadelphia: PA: Westminster Press, 1975), 113.

7   Mike Nappa, *God in Slow Motion: Reflections on Jesus and the 10 Unexpected Lessons You Can See in His Life* (Nashville, TN: Thomas Nelson, 2013), 93.

8   "A Far Country—Decapolis," http://followtherabbi.com/guide/detail/a-far-country-decapolis (accessed: March 20, 2015). Note: Some scholars believe Jesus may have had the Decapolis in mind in his parable about the prodigal son who went to a distant land and ended up eating with the pigs he was feeding (Luke 15:13-16).

9   Learn more about the ministry of the Navigators at http://www.navigators.org.

10   Robertson McQuilken, *Victorious Christian Living: A Biblical Exposition of Sanctification* (Columbia, SC: Columbia International University, 2008), 28.

11   Joanna Weaver, *Having a Mary Spirit* (Colorado Springs, CO: Waterbook Press, 2006), 236.

12   Alan Johnson, Romans: *The Freedom Letter, Vol. 1*, Everyman's Bible Commentary (Chicago, IL: Moody Press, 1984), 59.

13   Ronald Porter-Efron, *Rage: A Step-By-Step Guide to Overcoming Explosive Anger* (Oakland, CA: New Harbinger Publications, 2007), 12-13.

14   Francis Schaeffer, *The Mark of the Christian* (Downers Grove, IL: InterVarsity Press, 1970), 24.

15   Max Lucado, *The Applause of Heaven* (Dallas: Word, 1996), 100.

16   Andrew Murry, quoted in Paul Lee Tan, *Encyclopedia of 7,700 Illustrations: Signs of the Times* (Garland, TX: Bible Communications, 1996), 2304.

17   Larry Hopkins & Jason Hopkins, *Journey to a Fearless Life* (Fairfax, VA: Xulon Press, 2006), 251.

18   Perry Noble, *Overwhelmed: Winning the War Against Worry* (Carol Stream, IL: Tyndale House, 2014), 73-75.

19   Richard Blackaby, *Unlimiting God: Increasing Your Capacity to Experience the Divine* (Colorado Springs, CO: Multnomah Books, 2009), 125.

20   W.E. Vine, *An Expository Dictionary of New Testament Words* (Nashville, TN: Thomas Nelson, 1940), 159.

21   Phillip May, *Which Way to Educate* (Chicago, IL: Moody Press, 1975), 9.

22   Alexander Graham Bell, http://www.quoteyard.com/concentrate-all-your-thoughts-upon-the-work-at-hand-the-suns-rays-do-not-burn-until-brought-to-a-focus/ (accessed: March 20, 2015).

23   Rembrandt's "Simeon's Song of Praise" http://www.artbible.info/art/large/598.html (accessed: March 20, 2015). Eric Rennie, "Rembrandt's Last Painting" http://www.godwardweb.org/rembrandt%27slastp.html (accessed: February 13, 2015).

24   Tim LaHaye, *Jesus: Why the World Is Still Fascinated by Him* (Colorado Springs, CO: David C. Cook, 2009), 48.

25   Compassion. Dictionary.com. *Collins English Dictionary - Complete & Unabridged 10th Edition*. HarperCollins Publishers. http://dictionary.reference.com/browse/compassion (accessed: March 20, 2015).

26   Walter Elwell (ed), "Entry for Compassion." *Evangelical Dictionary of Theology* (Grand Rapids, MI: Baker Books, 1997).

27   Todd Marrah and Todd Hall, "Spiritual Formation: The Spiritual Lives of ACSI Students." *Christian School Education*, 14 (2011), 32.

28   Mike Nappa, *God in Slow Motion: Reflections on Jesus and the 10 Unexpected Lessons You Can See in His Life* (Nashville, TN: Thomas Nelson, 2013), 92.

29   Brother Lawrence, *The Practice of the Presence of God* (Uhrichsville, OH: Barbour and Company, 1993), 43.

30   Wess Stafford, *Just a Minute* (Chicago, IL: Moody Press, 2012), 190-192.

31   Navigator Bridge to Life, http://www.navigators.org/Tools/Evangelism%20Resources/Tools/The%20Bridge%20to%20Life (accessed: March 20, 2015).

32   Brother Lawrence, *The Practice of the Presence of God* (Uhrichsville, OH: Barbour and Company, 1993), 29.

33   W.E. Vine, *An Expository Dictionary of New Testament Words* (Nashville, TN: Thomas Nelson, 1940), 1020.

[34] Richard L. Pratt, Jr., *Pray With Your Eyes Open* (Phillipsburg, NJ: P&R Publishing, 1987), 20.

[35] Gangle, Kenneth, *Team Leadership in Christian Ministry: Using Multiple Gifts to Build a Unified Vision* (Chicago, IL: Moody Press, 1997), 59.

[36] Francis Assisi, quoted in J. Oswald Sanders, *Spiritual Leadership* (Chicago, IL: Moody Press, 1994), 30-31.

[37] Ruth Harms Calkin, "I Wonder" (posted on July 29, 2011), http://www.ruthcalkin.com (accessed: March 20, 2015). Used with permission.

[38] Clay Werner, *On the Brink: Grace for the Burned-Out Pastor* (Phillipsburg, NJ: P&R Publishing, 2014), 13.

[39] Michael Zigarelli, *Cultivating Christian Character* (Fairfax, VA: Xulon Press, 2002), 47.

[40] Oxford Dictionaries, s.v. "priority" accessed: March 20, 2015 http://www.oxforddictionaries.com/us/definition/american_english/priority (accessed: March 20, 2015).

[41] Alfred Edersheim, *The Life and Times of Jesus the Messiah*, Book IV (Grand Rapids, MI: Eerdmans Printing Company, 1981), 360.

[42] William Barclay, *The Letter to the Romans*, Daily Bible Study Series (Philadelphia: PA: Westminster Press, 1975), 74.

[43] (Ibid)

[44] Matthew Henry, *Commentary on the Whole Bible* (Grand Rapids, MI: Zondervan Publishing House, 1961)

[45] Billy Graham, *Peace with God* (Nashville, TN: W Publishing Group: 1984), 273.

[46] Clay Werner, *On the Brink: Grace for the Burned-Out Pastor* (Phillipsburg, NJ: P&R Publishing, 2014), 45.

[47] Walter Bradford Cannon, n.d. In Wikipedia. Retrieved March 20, 2015 from http://en.wikipedia.org/wiki/Walter_Bradford_Cannon

[48] Francis Schaeffer, *The Mark of the Christian* (Downers Grove, IL: InterVarsity Press, 1970), 35.

[49] William Barclay, *The Letters to the Philippians, Colossians, and Thessalonians*, Daily Bible Study Series (Philadelphia: PA: Westminster Press, 1975) 159.

[50] Lauren Cox, "Who Invented the Telescope?" http://www.space.com/21950-who-invented-the-telescope.html (accessed: March 20, 2015).

[51] Rene Descartes, http://www.aip.org/history/cosmology/tools/tools-first-telescopes.htm (accessed: March 20, 2015).

[52] James Foley, "Thirty Meter Telescope to be Most Powerful Telescope in History" http://www.natureworldnews.com/articles/3020/20130717/thirty-meter-telescope-powerful-history-video.htm (accessed: March 20, 2015).

[53] Max Lucado, *Next Door Savior* (Nashville, TN: W Publishing, 2003), 57.

[54] Alan Johnson, Romans: *The Freedom Letter*, Vol. 1, Everyman's Bible Commentary (Chicago, IL: Moody Press, 1984), 13-14.

55    Logan Thompson, "Roman Roads" *History Today*, Volume: 47 Issue: 2, 1997. http://www.historytoday.com/logan-thompson/roman-roads (accessed: March 20, 2015).

56    Mother Theresa, quoted at http://www.values.com/inspirational-quotes/4121-Stay-Where-You-Are-Find-Yo- (accessed: March 20, 2015).

57    Dale Carnegie, http://hopefaithprayer.com/hope/hope-quotes (accessed: March 20, 2015).

58    Dismayed. Hebrew Dictionary (Lexicon-Concordance) http://lexiconcordance.com/hebrew/2865.html (accessed: March 20, 2015)

59    Aubrey Johnson, *The Barnabas Factor: Realize Your Encouragement Potential* (Nashville, TN: Gospel Advocate, 2004) 19.

60    James Kouzes and Barry Posner, *Encouraging the Heart: A Leader's Guide to Rewarding and Recognizing Others* (San Francisco, CA: Jossy-Bass, 2003), 81.

61    Bill Hybels, *Axiom: Powerful Leadership Proverbs* (Grand Rapids, MI: Zondervan, 2008), 70.

62    The Metropolitan Museum of Art, http://www.metmuseum.org/exhibitions/listings/2014/tullio-lombardo-adam; Carol Vogel, "Recreating Adam from Hundreds of Fragments after the Fall" http://www.nytimes.com/2014/11/09/arts/design/recreating-adam-from-hundreds-of-fragments-after-the-fall.html (accessed: March 20, 2015).

63    Joy McCullough, *Kingdom Living in Your Classroom* (Colorado Springs: CO: Purposeful Design, 2008) 44-46.

64    Max Lucado, *A Gentle Thunder* (Nashville, TN: Thomas Nelson, 1995), 30.

65    W.E. Vine, *An Expository Dictionary of New Testament Words* (Nashville, TN: Thomas Nelson, 1940), 1216.

66    Alan Johnson, Romans: *The Freedom Letter, Vol. 2*, Everyman's Bible Commentary (Chicago, IL: Moody Press, 1984), 32.

67    Bill Hybels, *Axiom: Powerful Leadership Proverbs* (Grand Rapids, MI: Zondervan, 2008), 187.

68    Frank Gaebelein, *The Pattern of God's Truth: The Integration of Faith and Learning* (Winona Lake, IN: BMH Books, 1968), 49-50.

69    John Bunyan, *John Bunyan's The Pilgrim's Progress* (New York, NY: Longmans, Green and Company, 1916), 148.

70    Richard Blackaby, *Unlimiting God: Increasing Your Capacity to Experience the Divine* (Colorado Springs, CO: Multnomah Books, 2009), 16.

71    J. Oswald Sanders, *Spiritual Leadership* (Chicago, IL: Moody Press, 1994), 81-82.

72    Gustav Warneck, quoted in J. Oswald Sanders, *Spiritual Leadership* (Chicago, IL: Moody Press, 1994), 52.

73    Graham Greene, *The Power and the Glory* (London: William Heinemann, 1940. Reprint, New York: Penguin Books, 1982), 12.

74    Jeff Myers, *Handoff: The Only Way to Win the Race of Life* (Dayton, TN: Legacy Worldwide, 2008) 31.

75    Glen Schultz, *Kingdom Education: God's Plan for Educating Future Generations* (Nashville, TN: LifeWay Press, 2002), 125.

76    Richard Riesen, *Piety and Philosophy: A Primer for Christian Schools* (Colorado Springs, CO: Purposeful Design Publications), 93.

77    Daniel Egeler, *Mentoring Millennials: Shaping the Next Generation* (Colorado Springs, CO: NavPress, 2003), 23.

78    George Barna, *Transforming Children into Spiritual Champions* (Ventura, CA: Regal Books, 2003), 51.

79    Christopher Reel, excerpt taken from his blog while serving as a missionary in South Africa in 2010. Used with permission.